A LA Rules for Filing Catalog Cards

Prepared by the ALA Editorial Committee's Subcommittee
on the ALA Rules for Filing Catalog Cards

Pauline A. Seely
Chairman and Editor

Second Edition
Abridged

AMERICAN LIBRARY ASSOCIATION

Chicago 1968
CMenSP

Library of Congress Catalog Card Number 68–21020
Copyright © 1968 by the American Library Association
Manufactured in the United States of America

Preface

There have been many developments since the publication of the *A. L. A. Rules for Filing Catalog Cards* in 1942 that underscore the need for a new edition. There are new types of entries and new types of materials for which the earlier edition provides little or no guidance. Also, there has been a major restudy of rules for author and title entry, carried out by the Catalog Code Revision Committee of the American Library Association, which has culminated in a new edition of the *A. L. A. Cataloging Rules for Author and Title Entries*.[1] So that the publication of a new edition of the filing rules might be correlated with the new cataloging rules, in 1962 a Subcommittee on the A L A Rules for Filing Catalog Cards was established by the A L A Editorial Committee.

The Subcommittee has prepared both a full, detailed filing code and an abridgment of that code. The full version, a publication of 272 pages, offers a comprehensive coverage of filing problems, including much specialized and foreign material, as well as philosophical and descriptive notes pertaining to filing principles, correlation with cataloging rules, etc. The abridged edition presented herein consists of the same basic rules as the full version,

---

1. *Anglo-American Cataloging Rules*. Chicago, American Library Association, 1967.

but with most of the specialized and explanatory material omitted.[2] It should be adequate for the needs of most small and medium-sized general libraries, and also be useful as the basic tool for teaching filers in any size library.

The 1942 edition served as a summary of various methods of arrangement in that 60 percent of the rules gave alternatives. Because of the difficulties encountered in using that edition, and the many pleas for simpler rules that were received, it was decided that the new edition should be a consistent code of rules derived from one basic principle, with as few exceptions as possible.

The basic order recommended in this edition is the straight alphabetical, disregarding punctuation, with just a few exceptions, the major one being that personal surname entries are always arranged before other entries beginning with the same word or combination of words. This code combines for the first time all of the rules and suggestions for single-alphabet arrangements that appeared in the 1942 edition (except the interfiling of personal names), and shows the results of this principle when applied consistently throughout all the rules. From the filer's point of view, the simpler arrangements of the straight alphabetical order should result in more accurately filed catalogs; from the user's point of view, the inflexible order of the alphabet presents a uniform order that can be easily understood.

The filing arrangements in this edition are presented as the direct result of the form in which headings and entries are commonly made, based on standard cataloging rules and practice, without resorting to mental insertions, deletions, or transpositions. There are many instances where the rules in the new cataloging code, *Anglo-American Cataloging Rules,* are more effective from the filing viewpoint than the old rules, because either the resulting order of entries is better, or the present order is achieved more easily and directly. The Subcommittee on the A L A Rules for Filing Catalog Cards had the privilege of working with the Catalog Code Revision Committee with the mutual purpose of correlating author and title entries with filing order.

---

2. The main rule numbers in the Abridged Edition are the same as those in the full edition, but some of the subnumbers are different, due to omission of some of the specialized rules.

These filing rules are basically for a dictionary card catalog, and for manual filing. It may well be that the development of machine methods of filing will result in changes both in the form of entries and in their arrangement, in the not too distant future.

The Subcommittee wishes to thank all of the libraries that answered its questionnaires and so generously made copies of their filing rules available, also the many librarians who responded to questions and offered opinions, suggestions, etc.

Subcommittee on the
A L A Rules for Filing Catalog Cards
(of the A L A Editorial Committee)

VIRGINIA DREWRY	ORCENA MAHONEY PETERSON
DORALYN J. HICKEY	CLARIBEL SOMMERVILLE PROUDFIT
FRANCES R. LUBOVITZ	CATHARINE WHITEHORN

PAULINE A. SEELY, *Chairman*

Contents

PART I

Alphabetical arrangement

PART II

Order of entries

Explanatory notes on the text

Most of the examples are authentic entries that have been found in library catalogs or national bibliographies, the primary source being the Library of Congress printed catalogs.

Headings are usually given in Library of Congress cataloging form. Some are in the new form that will result from application of the 1967 *Anglo-American Cataloging Rules*. The new forms were used when it was known that they would be different from the old, and especially when the variation would affect the filing.

The headings in the examples are not always complete when completeness is not essential to illustrate the rule. For instance, dates are not usually included with names, forenames are not always given after surnames, nor is *see* added after all headings that are references, unless those elements are needed to illustrate the rule or to clarify the examples.

Subject headings are indicated by full capitals. Italics are not used for subheadings, etc. as they are in the *Anglo-American Cataloging Rules* and on Library of Congress cards. Such typography would have no effect on the filing.

Basic principle and basic order

BASIC PRINCIPLE

Filing should be straightforward, item by item through the entry, not disregarding or transposing any of the elements, nor mentally inserting designations. In the following rules there are only a few situations where this principle is not applied: these are usually due to the structure of the heading.

BASIC ORDER

1) The basic order is alphabetical, word by word, except in certain areas where a numerical or chronological arrangement is preferable.

2) When the same word, or combination of words, is used as the heading of different kinds of entry, the entries are arranged alphabetically word by word, disregarding kind of entry, form of heading, and punctuation, except that personal surname entries are arranged before other entries beginning with the same word or combination of words.

1

PART I

Alphabetical arrangement (Rules 1–18)

This part covers the rules for determining the alphabetical position of, or point of access for, all types of headings.

BASIC RULES (RULES 1–4)

1. Basic alphabeting rule

A. Alphabet. Arrange all entries, both English and foreign, alphabetically according to the order of the English alphabet.

B. Word by word. Arrange word by word, alphabeting letter by letter within the word. Begin with the first word on the first line, then go to the next word, etc. Apply the principle of "nothing before something," considering the space between words as "nothing." Thus, a single letter or shorter word precedes a longer word beginning with the same letter or letters. When two or more headings begin with the same word, arrange next by the first different word.

Every word in the entry is regarded, including articles, prepositions, and conjunctions, but initial articles are disregarded.

Example:

I met a man
Im Wandel der Jahre
Image books
Image of America
Images of America
Imaginary conversations
In an unknown land
In the days of giants
Inca

C. Dictionary catalog. In a dictionary catalog, interfile all types of entries (author, title, subject, series, etc.) and their related references, in one general alphabet.

2. Modified letters

Disregard the modification of all letters. This includes umlauts and all kinds of accents and diacritical marks in foreign languages.

Examples:

Muel, Léon
Muellen, Abraham
Muenscher, Joseph
Mullen, Allen
Müllen, Gustav
Mullen, Pat

Rolston, Brown
Rølvaag, Ole Edvart
Rolyat, Jane

3. Punctuation marks

Disregard punctuation marks that are part of a title or corporate name.

For punctuation in relation to order of entries under the same word, see Rule 19 and the specific rules for name entries, author and subject arrangement, etc.

Examples:

Life
Life—a bowl of rice
"Life after death"
Life, its true genesis
Life of . . . Frances Schlatter
Life! physical and spiritual

American Association for Health and Physical Education
American Association for Health, Physical Education, and
     Recreation
American Association for International Conciliation

4. Articles

A. Initial articles. Disregard an initial article in all languages and file by the word following it. In English the articles are "A," "An," and "The." For a list of initial articles to be disregarded in filing, see Appendix.

An exception to this rule is certain foreign proper names beginning with an article (see Rules 14 and 15).

Caution: Thought must be given to any short initial word, especially in foreign languages, where the same word may serve not only as an article but also as some other part of speech.

Examples:

A apple pie
A travers la France
Apache
An April after
Aquarium
L'art des jardins
Artists

Man and boy
The man of his time
Man of mark
A man of the age
Man of the world
Les misérables

Une des terres inconnues   ⸢Une = One⸥
Unemployed

B. Articles within the entry. All articles occurring within a title
or a heading are to be regarded, except those that actually are
initial articles in an inverted position or at the beginning of a
subdivision.

Examples:

Work for a man
Work for Julia
Work for the beginner

Stassen, Harold Edward
STATE, THE
STATE AND CHURCH

AGRICULTURE—U. S.
AGRICULTURE—THE WEST
AGRICULTURE—WYOMING

ABBREVIATED FORMS (RULES 5–9)

5. Initials

A. Arrange initials, single or in combination, as one-letter
words, before longer words beginning with the same initial letter,
wherever they occur in an entry. Interfile entries consisting of
initials plus words with entries consisting of initials only.

B. Arrange initials standing for names of organizations as
initials, not as abbreviations, i. e., not as if spelled in full.

C. Arrange inverted initials standing for authors' names alphabetically with other initials, disregarding the inversion and the
punctuation.

Examples for 5A-C:

A.
A. A.
AAAA
AAA Foundation for Traffic Safety

5

AAAS Conference on Science Teaching . . .
AACE
A., A. J. G.
AAUN news
"A" and "B" mandates
A., André C. H., *see* . . .
A apple pie
A. B.
The ABC about collecting
A B C and X Y Z
A. B. C. programs
A., J
A was an archer
Aa, Pieter van der
Aabel, Marie

I (For examples of I see p. 22)

UHF television
U. N., *see* United Nations
U. N. diary
U. N. E. C. A.   ⌊reference⌋
UN headquarters
U. N. I. C. E. F.   ⌊reference⌋
The UN record
U. S. O.
U–2 INCIDENT, 1960   ⌊U–TWO⌋
Uarov, M. I.

D. Different entries under same initials—Subarrangement.
Subarrange entries consisting of the same initials alphabetically
by title, according to the regular rules for order of entries.

Example:

> M.
> The Dayspring of youth, by M.

> M.

>> Letters from three continents
>> *see* Ward, Mathew Flournoy

>> "M."

> Thence and hence.

E. Acronyms

Preliminary note. An acronym is a brief form of a corporate name or term made up of a group of letters that are commonly written and/or spoken as a word. Examples: NATO, EURATOM, SACLANT, FORTRAN.
Arrange acronyms as words, unless written in all capitals with a space or period between the letters (e. g., U N E S C O; U. N. E. S. C. O.), which forms are to be filed as initials. If uncertain whether the initials are commonly spoken as a word, treat them as initials.

Examples:

U. D. F.
U. N. E. S. C. O., *see* . . .
U. R. S. S.
Unemployment
Unesco
UNESCO bibliographical handbooks
Unesco fellowship handbook
Ungar, Frederick

F. O. B. Detroit
F. O. R. T. R. A. N., *see* FORTRAN (COMPUTER PROGRAM LANGUAGE) (FORTRAN filed as a word)
F. P. A.

Forton, Jean
FORTRAN (COMPUTER PROGRAM LANGUAGE)
Fortress

6. Abbreviations

A. Arrange abbreviations as if spelled in full in the language of the entry, except "Mrs.," which is filed as written.

Examples:

Doctor at sea
Dr. Christian's office
Doctor come quickly
Doktor Brents Wandlung
Dr. Mabuse der Spieler   ɾDoktorɹ
Doktor Mamlocks Ausweg

7

MISSIONS
Missis Flinders   ₍filed as spelled₎
Mister Abbott
Mr. Adam
Mister Barney Ford
Mistress, *see also* entries beginning with "Mrs.," filed under
    that spelling
Mistress Anne
Monsieur et Madame Curie
M. & Mme. Lhomme   ₍Monsieur et Madame₎
Monsieur et Madame Moloch
Mr.
        Entries beginning with the above abbreviation are
    filed as if spelled "Mister."
Mrs., *see also* entries beginning with "Mistress"
Mrs. Miniver
M'sieu Gustave   ₍filed as spelled₎
Much

B. Abbreviations of geographical names. Arrange initials and
other abbreviations for geographical names in author and subject
headings, and in titles and other entries if the full name of the
place for which they stand is commonly known, as if written in full.

Examples:

Concord, Mass.
Concord saunterer
Concord, Vt.
Concord, Va.

The great Brink's holdup
Gt. Brit.   Office of Commonwealth Relations
Gt. Brit. on trial
Great Britain or little England?

U. S. (For examples of U. S. see p. 54)

C. Subject subdivision abbreviations. If subject subdivisions
are abbreviated in subject headings as they commonly are in
the tracing, arrange them as if written in full.

Example:

U. S.—FOREIGN POPULATION
U. S.—FOR. REL.   [FOREIGN RELATIONS]
U. S. foreign trade policy

7. Elisions, possessives, etc.

Arrange elisions, contractions, and possessives as written. Do not supply missing letters. Disregard the apostrophe and treat as one word any word or contraction of two words that contains an apostrophe, unless the apostrophe is followed by a space.

Examples:

Boys and girls at school
Boys' and girls' book of indoor games
The boys' book of airships
Boy's book of body building
Boys will be boys

East o' the sun and west o' the moon
East of Eden
East of the sun and west of the moon

Who is who in music
Whoa, Grandma!
Who'd be a doctor?
Whodunit?
Whom God hath joined
Who's who
Whose love was the greater?

Bibliothèque d'art
Bibliothèque de la Fondation Thiers
Bibliothèque de l'Usine
Bibliothèque d'histoire

8. Signs and symbols

A. Signs in titles. Disregard signs, such as • • • or ——, at the beginning of or within titles and arrange by the word following the signs.

Example:
And another thing
——and beat him when he sneezes
And now good-bye
And so **. . .** accounting
And they shall walk

B. Ampersand. Arrange the ampersand (&) as "and," "et," "und," etc., according to the language in which it is used.

Examples:
Art and beauty
Art & commonsense
ART AND INDUSTRY

L'art et la beauté
L'art & la guerre
L'art et les artistes

C. Signs and symbols spoken as words. Arrange signs and symbols that are ordinarily spoken as words as if they were written out, in the context of the title, in the language of the rest of the title.

Examples:	*File as:*
$2 \times 2 = 5$	Two times two equals five
3×3: Stairway to the sea	Three by three . . .
% of gain	Percent of gain
$$$ and sense	Dollars and sense
$20 a week	Twenty dollars a week

9. Numerals

For numerals and dates that indicate a sequence see Rule 36.

A. General rule. Arrange numerals in the titles of books, corporate names, cross references, etc. as if spelled out in the language of the entry. Spell numerals and dates as they are spoken, placing "and" before the last element in compound numbers in English, except in a decimal fraction where the "and" must be omitted.

1. Basic table. The following table gives examples of basic numerals and their corresponding words in English for filing as numbers and as dates.

	Number	Date
100	One hundred	One hundred
101	One hundred and one	One hundred one
1000	One thousand	One thousand
⎰1001–	One thousand and one–	⎰One thousand one–
⎱1999	One thousand nine hundred and ninety-nine	⎱Nineteen ninety-nine
	except round thousands, e. g.	
⎰1100	Eleven hundred	⎰Eleven hundred
⎱1600	Sixteen hundred	⎱Sixteen hundred
15,210	Fifteen thousand, two hundred and ten	
6½	Six and a half	

2. Special usages. Examples of numerals used in special ways, as addresses, time of day, shortened dates.

Examples:	*File as:*
112 Elm Street	One twelve
1000 Chestnut St.	Ten hundred
5:30 to midnight	Five-thirty
'49 to '94	Forty-nine to ninety-four

Examples for 9A:

One America	
One half the people	
One hundred, *see also* entries beginning with "Hundred"	
100 American poems	⌜one hundred⌝
150 science experiments step-by-step	⌜one hundred and fifty⌝
One hundred and five sonnets	
101 best games for teen-agers	⌜one hundred and one⌝
130 feet down	⌜one hundred and thirty⌝
130,000 kilowatt power station	⌜one hundred and thirty thousand⌝
103 simple transistor projects	⌜one hundred and three⌝
One hundred best books	
100,000 years of daily life	⌜one hundred thousand⌝
100 to dinner	⌜one hundred⌝
One is only human	
1,999 belly laughs	⌜one thousand nine hundred and ninety-nine⌝

112 Elm Street   ⌜one twelve⌟
One's, two's, three's

Twenty-four hours
2400 business books   ⌜twenty-four hundred⌟
Twenty-four portraits

Nineteen centuries of Christian song
1918, the last act   ⌜nineteen eighteen⌟
Nineteen eighty-four
The 1950's come first   ⌜nineteen fifties⌟
The 1956 Presidential campaign   ⌜nineteen fifty-six⌟
1943 war job guide for women   ⌜nineteen forty-three⌟
1940–1942 ⌜poem⌟   ⌜nineteen forty to nine-
                                                teen forty-two⌟

Europe since 1815   ⌜eighteen fifteen⌟
Europe since 1500   ⌜fifteen hundred⌟
Europe since Napoleon
Europe since 1789   ⌜seventeen eighty-nine⌟
Europe since the war

Dix, Morgan
10 ans de politique sociale en Pologne   ⌜dix⌟
Dix ans d'études historiques
1915; revue de guerre en deux actes   ⌜dix neuf cent quinze⌟
Dix vues de Lisbonne

Hundert Jahre grieschische Landwirtschaft
100 Jahre italienischer Geschichte   ⌜hundert⌟
150 kleine Gärten   ⌜hundertfünfzig⌟
Der hundertjährige Calender

    B. Numerals following given names in titles. Arrange a numeral
following a given name in a title as if spelled out in the language
of the rest of the title, as spoken. In English the numeral is read
as an ordinal preceded by "the." For numerals in given name
headings see Rule 25.

12

Example:

The Henry James reader
Henry V, King of England, 1387–1422
　　　　　　　　　　　ʟHenry King of England, 5ᴉ
Henry VIII, King of England, 1491–1547
　　　　　　　　　　　ʟHenry King of England, 8ᴉ
HENRY MOUNTAINS, UTAH

Henry VIII　　　　　　　　ʟHenry the Eighthᴉ
Shakespeare, William

Henry VIII and his wives　　　ʟHenry the Eighthᴉ
Henry VIII's fifth wife　　　　ʟHenry the Eighth'sᴉ

Henry V　　　　　　　　　　ʟHenry the Fifthᴉ
Shakespeare, William

Henry, the uncatchable mouse

C. Names of things that include a numeral. Arrange the names of classes of aircraft, boats, etc. in which a numeral is an integral part of the heading alphabetically as spoken.

Example:

B. F. V.
B–58 BOMBER　　　　　　　　　　　　　　ʟfifty-eightᴉ
B–58 HUSTLER (BOMBERS) *see* B–58 BOMBER
B. G.
B–17 BOMBER　　　　　　　　　　　　　　ʟseventeenᴉ
Baab, August

VARIANT FORMS (RULES 10–12)

Introductory notes. Rules 10 and 11 recommend interfiling of the same words spelled differently and of the same compound words written differently, when more than one form appears in the catalog. For words spelled differently a choice must be made, according to the criteria given below; two-word (or hyphened) forms are always filed under the one-word form. Rule 12 recommends that dialect, colloquial, and humorous forms be arranged as written.

13

When there is an established subject heading or subject cross reference under one of the spellings, choose that spelling (e. g., "Archaeology" rather than "Archeology," but "Encyclopedia" rather than "Encyclopaedia").

In other cases generally choose the most commonly accepted current usage. Consult the latest edition of standard general dictionaries.

When there is a choice between the American and English spellings, choose the American (e. g., "Color," rather than "Colour").

Choose the modern rather than the archaic spelling (e. g., "Complete" rather than "Compleat," "Mechanic" rather than "Mechanick").

DIFFERENT PARTS OF SPEECH

When there are several parts of speech based on the same word, the spelling or form chosen for the basic word will apply to all (e. g., "Coloured," "Colouring," "Colours," will file as though spelled "Colored," "Coloring," "Colors"), even though some of the words may appear only in the unused form.

REFERENCES FROM VARIANT FORMS

Explanatory references should always be made from the form or forms not chosen, and an explanatory note made under the form chosen.

10. Words spelled in different ways

When different entries, including corporate names, begin with or contain the same word spelled in different ways (e. g., Color and Colour), choose one spelling, according to the criteria given in the introduction to this section, and file all entries under that spelling. If there is only one of the possible spellings in the catalog, generally file it as spelled, without references, until such time as the other spelling appears.

Example:

Color

> Here are filed all entries beginning with the words "Color" and "Colour."

COLOR

Colour harmony in dress

Color harmony spectrum

Colorado

COLORED GLASS, *see* . . .

Coloured glasses

Colours of good and evil

Colors: what they can do for you

The colossus again

Colour

> For entries beginning with the above word see the spelling "Color."

Colowick, Sidney P

11. Words written in different ways

A. Basic rule—for compound words that appear in the catalog in only one form

1. Arrange hyphened words as separate words when the parts are complete words, i.e., when each part can stand alone as a word in the context of the combined word (e. g., Epoch-making, but not Co-operative). The hyphen is treated as a space for filing purposes and arrangement is word by word.

Example:

An epoch in life insurance

Epoch-making papers in United States history

The epoch of reform

2. Arrange as two words compound words that are written as two separate words.

3. Arrange as one word compound words that are written as one.

B. Same word written differently. In the case of compound words that appear in the catalog written both as two separate words (or hyphened) and as a single word, interfile all entries, including corporate names, under the one-word form. This applies to subject headings and subject cross references also.

Examples:

Home carpentry

Home coming

>   For entries beginning with the above words, written with or without a hyphen, see the one-word form "Homecoming."

Home cookery

Homebrew and patches

Homecoming

>   Here are filed all entries beginning with the words "Homecoming," "Home coming," and "Home-coming."

Homecoming

Bradbury, Ray

The home-coming

Doyle, Sir Arthur Conan

Homecoming

Seifert, Elizabeth

Homecrafts in Sweden

Camp dramatics

Camp fire

>   For entries beginning with the above words, written with or without a hyphen, see the one-word form "Campfire."

Camp grub

Campbell

Campfire

>   Here are filed all entries beginning with the words "Campfire," Camp fire," and "Camp-fire."

Campfire adventure stories

Camp-fire and cotton-field

Camp Fire Girls

The Campfire girls flying around the globe

CAMPFIRE PROGRAMS

CAMPING

SEA POETRY

Sea power

>   For entries beginning with the above words, written

with or without a hyphen, see the one-word form
"Seapower."
A sea ringed with visions
Seaports and people of Europe
Seapower
> Here are filed all entries beginning with the words
> "Seapower," "Sea power," and "Sea-power."
SEA-POWER
Sea power in the machine age
Seapower in the nuclear age
Sea-power in the Pacific
Search

C. Combining forms

1. Arrange as one word, words beginning with a prefix or combining form such as anti-, bi-, co-, electro-, ex-, inter-, pan-, post-, etc. (i. e., words in which the first part cannot stand alone as a word with the meaning it has in the combined word), whether written with a hyphen, as two separate words, or as one word. Interfile all the variant forms of a word, including corporate names, in one alphabetical file.

Example:
  Post, Wiley
  Post-
> Words beginning with the above combining forms are
> alphabetized as one word.
  Post biographies of famous journalists
  POST-ROADS
  POSTAGE-STAMPS
  POST-IMPRESSIONISM (ART)
  Post-war British cars
  Postwar British fiction
  The post-war condition of Britain

2. Combining forms made from the names of countries and peoples (e. g., Anglo-, Franco-, Greco-, etc.) are an exception. These are filed as separate words before longer words beginning with the same letters.

Example:

Franco, Victor
Franco-American Audio-Visual Distribution Center, New
York
Franco Bahamonde, Francisco
FRANCO-SPANISH WAR, 1635–1659
Francoeur, Robert Alfred

12. Dialect, colloquial, humorous forms

Arrange words in dialect, colloquial, and humorous forms and
spellings as written. This includes the forms "de" and "ye" when
used as articles for effect, even as initial articles.

Examples:

De natura deorum
De night in de front
Delzons, Louis
Dem good old times
Demachy, Edouard
R. F. R.
℞ for slimming   ₁filed as R₁
R. Y. A.
'R' you listenin', by Tony Wons
R. Z. T.
Ye gods and little fishes
Ye olden time
Yea and nay
Yeager, George

NAMES—ALPHABETIZATION
(RULES 13–18)

This section covers the alphabeting rules for special types of
proper names, both personal and geographical. For details of arrangement of entries under proper names, see Rules 20-25, Personal name entry arrangement.

13. Compound proper names

Arrange compound proper names (i. e., names consisting of two or more separate words, with or without a hyphen) as separate words. Alphabet with regard to all words in the name, including articles, conjunctions, and prepositions within the name.

Examples:

Hall Co., Tex.
Hall-Edwards,
Hall of fame
Hall Williams,
Hallam,

Martin-Dairvault,
Martín de Almagro,
Martín de la Escalera,
Martín del Campe,
Martin Deslandes,

New Jersey
A new way of life
New York
Newark

Saint among the Hurons
Saint-Gaudens,
St. Petersburg
Saint Vincent
Saintaux,
Sainte-Beuve,
Saintes,
San Antonio
San Francisco
Sanborn

14. Proper names with a prefix

Preliminary note. A name with a prefix is one that begins with a separately written particle consisting of an article (e. g., La Crosse), a preposition (e. g., De Morgan), a combination of a preposition and an article (e. g., Del Mar, Van der Veer), or a

19

term which originally expressed relationship (e. g., O'Brien), with
or without a space, hyphen, or apostrophe between the prefix and
the name.

A. Arrange proper names with a prefix as one word.

Examples:

De senectute
De Alberti, Amelia
Defoe,
De la Roche,
Delaware
Del Mar, Eugene

Elagin, Ivan
EL ALAMEIN, BATTLE OF, 1942   ₁Arabic place name₁[3]
Elam, Elizabeth
El Dorado, Ark.   ₁Spanish place name₁
Eldorado, Neb.
El-Wakil, Mohamed Mohamed   ₁Arabic personal name₁
Elwell,

Obrie,
O'Brien,
Obrig,

Vanderbilt,
Van der Veer, Judy
Van Derveer, Lettie C.
Vanderwalker,
Vander Zanden,

B. M', Mc, Mac. Arrange names beginning with the prefixes **M'**
and **Mc** as if written **Mac**.

Examples:

Mach,
McHenry,
Machinery
MacHugh,
Machuron,

---

3. For the Arabic names see Rule 15A2.

Maclaren, Ian
MacLaren, J
M'Laren, J   Wilson
McLaren, Jack
MacLaren, James

15. Oriental names

A. Islamic and Hebrew names

1. Uncapitalized initial articles. Disregard the uncapitalized initial articles "al-" or "el-" prefixed with a hyphen to Arabic, etc. names, and the articles "ha-" or "he-" prefixed to Hebrew names.

Example:
Jund, Trinedad
al-Jundī, Ad'ham
June

2. Capitalized "Al" and "El." "Āl" at the beginning of an Arabic name is to be regarded and filed as a separate word. "Al" and "El" (capitalized), with or without a hyphen, are to be regarded but treated as prefixes, the name being filed as one word.

Examples:
Al Sherman Enterprises, New York
Āl Waṣfī Waṣfī
Alabama

Aljian, George W
AL JIB, JORDAN
Alken, Henry Thomas

El (For examples of El see p. 20)

3. Parts of a name. When an Islamic or Hebrew name begins with a part expressing relationship (e. g., the Arabic "Abd, Abu, Ibn"; the Hebrew "Ben"; the Syriac "Bar") alphabet under the prefix. Treat each part of a name, including articles within a name, as a separate word.

Example:
Abū 'Abd Allāh Muhammad
Abū 'Abdallāh Harīth ibn Asad

Abu al-Walīd Marwān ibn Janāḥ
Abū ʿAlī al-Hasan
Abū Saʿīd
Abud, Salomón

B. Chinese and Japanese names
1. Arrange Chinese and Japanese names by the first part (i. e., the family name) whether it is separated from the rest of the name by a comma or not.
2. An old Chinese name that consists of only two hyphened syllables (e. g., Lao-tzǔ, meaning the Old one) is arranged as a two-word phrase.

Example for 15B1-2:

Chen, Chen Chong
Chen Chi
Ch'ên, Ch'i, fl. 1773
Ch'ên, Chi-t'ung
Ch'ên, Chia-kan
Chen Huan-Chang
Chen, Jack
Chen, Wei
Chên-chu
Chên-chung, pseud.
Chen Tsen I, Pierre Claver
Chenault, John Cabell

3. **Exception to the general rules.** It is recommended that all entries beginning with "I" be interfiled word by word in one straight alphabetical file, disregarding punctuation, kind of entry, language, etc. The same policy is recommended for the letter "U," which appears both as a Chinese surname and as a Burmese name and title of address.

Example:

IAA	
I, a stranger	[title]
I AM MOVEMENT	
I, An	[name]
I, Anastasia	[title]
I can wait	[title]

I, Chih
I-ching, 635-713   ⌐name⌐
I ching   ⌐uniform title⌐
I, Claudius   ⌐title⌐
Iams, Jack

16. American Indian names

Arrange hyphenated American Indian names as one word.

Example:
Absalom's conspiracy
Ab-sa-ra-ka, home of the Crows
Absaroka Mountains, Ky.

17. Nicknames and sobriquets

A. Treat nicknames and sobriquets as words, not as personal names. Disregard an initial article and file by the word following it.

Example:
Gréciano,
El Greco, d. 1614
Grecu,

B. References. A reference should be made to file under the article. Consider the article a prefix and file as one word under the article.

Example:
Elgozy,
El Greco, *see* El Greco, d. 1614 (filed under Greco)
Elgström,

18. Proper names spelled differently

Arrange separately proper names that differ in spelling, however slightly.

Examples:
Andersen, Hans Christian
Anderson, Arthur
Anderssen, Adolf
Andersson, Axel

Catharina, Saint, of Alexandria
Catharine II, Empress of Russia
Cather, Willa Sibert
Catherine de Médici, consort of Henry II, King of France
Katharine, pseud.
Katherine of Aragon

Allegany Co., Md.
Alleghany Mountains
Allegheny Co., Pa.

PART II

*Order of entries
(Rules 19-37)*

This part covers the rules for the order of different kinds of
entries beginning with the same word.

19. Order of entries under same word—General rules

A. When the same word, or combination of words, is used as
the heading of different kinds of entry, arrange the entries in two
main groups as follows:

1) Single surname entries, arranged alphabetically by forenames
2) All other entries, arranged alphabetically word by word,
   disregarding kind of entry, form of heading, and punctuation

B. Arrange subject entries under a personal or corporate name
immediately after the author entries for the same name.

C. Interfile title added entries and subject entries that are
identical and subarrange alphabetically by their main entries.

Example for Rule 19:
   Love, John L.
   LOVE, JOHN L.
   Love, William

      Love   [title]
   Bowen, Elizabeth

      LOVE
   Magoun, F. Alexander

      Love   [title]
   Mamis, Justin

   Love and beauty
   LOVE, MATERNAL
   LOVE POETRY
   LOVE—QUOTATIONS, MAXIMS, ETC.
   Love songs, old and new
   LOVE (THEOLOGY)
   Love your neighbor

PERSONAL NAME ENTRY ARRANGEMENT
(RULES 20–25)

This section covers the rules for the filing position of personal name entries in relation to other entries in the catalog and to each other.

20. Surname entries—General rules

Preliminary note. A surname in a personal name entry is the part that precedes the first comma in the entry, except when that name is a given name.

A. Filing position. A surname entry precedes all other entries beginning with the same word or combination of words. A single surname is always the first entry under that word. In relation to other entries in the catalog consider only the surname, not the forenames or designations.

B. Order of entries under the same surname—General rule. Arrange headings of the same surname in groups in the following order:

1) Surname alone with nothing following it
2) Surname alone followed only by dates
3) Surname followed by designation, forenames, or initials

C. Order of entries under the same surname followed by designations, forenames, or initials

1. Arrange entries under the same surname followed by designations, forenames, or initials alphabetically by the designation, forename, or initial that follows the surname, all in one group.

2. An initial precedes a fully written forename beginning with the same initial letter.

D. Order of entries when surname and forenames are the same

1. Arrange headings of the same surname and forenames in groups in the following order:

1) Names with neither dates nor designations
2) Names with designations (whether at end or within the entry) but no dates
3) Names with dates, or designations and dates

2. Arrange the same names without dates but with designations, such as titles of nobility, honor or address, or distinguishing phrases, alphabetically by the designations preceding or following the forenames.

3. Arrange the same names with dates chronologically by the first date given, whether it is a birth date, approximate date, or death date.

4. When a name has both dates and some kind of designation disregard the designation unless needed to distinguish between entries otherwise identical.

Comprehensive example for Rule 20:[4]

    Smith,
    Smith,   fl. 1641
    Smith, Adam

---

4. Because no one surname would present actual examples of every situation, some forenames, titles, designations, and dates have arbitrarily been added to the surname Smith.

Smith, Captain
Smith, Chester Lloyd
Smith, Lord George
Smith, J
Smith, J   A   X
Smith, J   Alden
Smith, J   B
Smith, Jack Hayden
Smith, John
Smith, John, LL. D.
Smith, Mrs. John
Smith, John, pseud.
Smith, Sir John
Smith, John, surgeon and trading captain
Smith, John, 1563–1616
Smith, John, Bp. of Chester, 1613?–1686
Smith, John, fl. 1747
Smith, John, 1747–1807
Smith, John, 1797?–1837
Smith, John, 1798–1888
Smith, John, b. 1823
Smith, John, d. 1827
Smith, John, ca. 1837–1896
Smith, John, 1837–1922
Smith, Mrs. John, 1847–1935
Smith, John, d. 1861
Smith (John) and Son, ltd.
Smith, John A
Smith, Mr.   [Mr.=Mister]
Smith, Mitchell
Smith, Mrs.   [Mrs.=Mrs.]
Smith, pseud.
Smith, William
Smith   [fiction title]
Smith and Jones   [fiction title]
Smith College

SPECIAL TYPES OF SURNAME ENTRIES
(RULES 21-24)

21. Compound surname entries

Interfile compound surname entries alphabetically with the group of titles, etc. following entries for the first part of the name alone as a single surname. Alphabet with regard to all words in the surname part of the entry. For examples see Comprehensive examples for Rules 21 and 22, below.

22. Names of clan, family, house, dynasty, etc.

Interfile a surname followed by "family," "House of," etc., alphabetically with the group of titles, etc. following all surname entries under the same name. Alphabet with regard to all words in the heading, disregarding the comma in an inverted heading.

Comprehensive examples for Rules 21 and 22:

Lloyd, William
Lloyd Brothers, Cincinnati
LLOYD FAMILY
Lloyd George, David
Lloyd George Adams Library
LLOYD GEORGE FAMILY
Lloyd guide to Australia
Lloyd-Williams, Richard
Lloyd's of London

Gil, Peter Paul
Gil-Albert, Juan
Gil Blas   [title]
Gil de Rubio, Victor M
Gil Munilla, Ladislav
Gil-Robles, Enrique
Gil-Robles y Quiñones, José María
Gil Vicente   [title]
Gil y Pablos, Francisco
Gil Yépez, Carlos
GILA RIVER

Medici, Lorenzo de', il Magnifico
The Medici art series
MEDICI, HOUSE OF
Medici-Tornaquinci, Alfonso Cosimo de'

23. Corporate name entries beginning with a surname

A. Surname followed by forenames, etc. Arrange a corporate
name consisting of a surname followed by forenames, etc. in its
alphabetical place among the personal names in the surname
group.

B. Surname without forenames or initials. Arrange a corporate
name consisting of a surname only, followed by a designation,
and compound and phrase names in their alphabetical place in
the group of titles, etc. following all surname entries under the
same name. Alphabet with regard to all words in the heading, including "inc.," "ltd.," etc., and such phrases as "and Company,"
"(Firm)," etc.

Examples for Rule 23:
Fraser, Alice
Fraser, Arthur, 1893–
Fraser (Arthur) and Company
Fraser, Charles
Fraser & Charles
FRASER FAMILY
Fraser (Firm)
Fraser-Knight, James
The Fraser murder case
Fraser, Smith, and Company

Prentice, William Reed
The prentice
Prentice-Hall book about inventions
Prentice-Hall, inc.
Prentice-Hall world atlas

24. Place name followed by a personal name or personal title

Arrange entries for noblemen and prelates which consist of a
place name combined with personal names or a designation

among the personal surnames, not with places. Subarrange alphabetically by the personal names or designation in the entry.

Examples:

Essex, Arthur
Essex, Arthur Capel, 1st Earl of
Essex, Richard Hamilton
Essex [place, titles, etc.]

Ely, Alfred
Ely, Bishop of, 1506–1515, *see* Stanley, James, Bp. of Ely, 1465?–1515
Ely, Ezra Stiles
Ely, Francis Turner, Bp. of, *see* Turner, Francis, Bp. of Ely
Ely, Frank David
Ely [place, titles, etc.] .

25. Given name entries

A. General rules relating to form of headings

1. Disregard a numeral following a given name except when necessary to distinguish between given names with the same designation. Arrange first alphabetically by the designation, then when there is more than one numeral, numerically by the numeral.

Example:

Charles V, Emperor of Germany
Charles II, King of France
Charles I, King of Great Britain
Charles II, King of Great Britain

2. Disregard a second given name or family name that comes *between* a numeral and a designation and alphabet by the designation; but if the second name *precedes* the numeral, consider as a compound given name and alphabet by the second name.

Examples:

Gustaf Adolf, crown prince of Sweden
Gustaf-Janson, Gösta
Gustaf I Vasa, King of Sweden
Gustaf II Adolf, King of Sweden
Gustaf III, King of Sweden
Gustaf, Prince of Sweden and Norway

Victor Chemical Works
Victor Emmanuel II, King of Italy
Victor Gaunt, master spy

B. Filing position of given name entries and order of entries under the same given name

1. Arrange all given name entries, both single and compound, after the single surname entries of the same name, interfiling alphabetically in the group of titles, etc. beginning with the same word. Alphabet with regard to all designations and words, articles and prepositions included, and disregard punctuation.

2. When an ordinal numeral follows a given name in a title entry, arrange it as spoken, according to Rule 9B.

Comprehensive examples for Rule 25:

Charles, William
Charles   ₍title₎
Charles Ann, Sister
Charles Auchester   ₍title₎
Charles, Brother
Charles City, Iowa
Charles, Count of Valois
Charles de Blois
Charles, Duke of Burgundy
Charles II, Duke of Parma
Charles Edward, the Young Pretender
CHARLES FAMILY
Charles III, King of France
Charles I, King of Great Britain
Charles II, King of Great Britain
The Charles men
Charles-Roux, François
Charles the Bold, *see* Charles, Duke of Burgundy
Charles the Second   ₍title₎
Charles II and his court   ₍Charles the second₎
CHARLES W. MORGAN (SHIP)

Homer, Winslow
Homer
Homer and history

AUTHOR ENTRY ARRANGEMENT
(RULES 26–27)

Introductory notes

DIFFERENT METHODS OF ARRANGEMENT

There are two different basic arrangements for titles under an author: (1) alphabetical by title page titles, or (2) organized, in which the collected works and selections are grouped and all editions and translations of a particular work are brought together. Arrangement of all works by title page title is suitable only for a small collection with relatively few titles under an author. An organized arrangement should be introduced in situations where the alphabetic order becomes difficult to consult because of the number and character of the titles, editions, translations, etc., as under classic and voluminous authors, and where the collection is used for research purposes.

Rule 26 covers the basic alphabetic arrangement under an author entry, including general rules that are applicable in Rule 27 also.

Rule 27 covers situations where a uniform title is applied in order to secure a special organized arrangement of the titles, editions, and translations.

EDITIONS

Libraries have varied widely in methods of arranging editions of the same title. Some of the systems in use are as follows:
1) Scientific, technical, and other factual material—by date, often in reverse order with latest edition first
2) Belles-lettres—alphabetical by name of publisher, editor, translator, illustrator, series, etc., either consistently by one of them or by whichever is most appropriate in a particular case
3) All types of material by date of publication, either with earliest date first or with latest date first

33

The following rules recommend the chronological order for all types of material and the straight rather than the reverse order of dates. This system will be more effective, especially in public libraries where many copies are added, if reprint dates are disregarded in cataloging.

26. General arrangement under author

A. Basic rule. Under an author heading arrange different kinds of entries in groups in the following order:

1) Works *by* the author, subarranged alphabetically by their titles
2) Works *about* the author, without subdivision, subarranged alphabetically by their main entries; except subject entries for individual works, which are arranged in group 1 immediately after the author entries for the same work (see 26B11 below)
3) Works *about* the author, with subdivision, subarranged alphabetically by the subdivisions

B. Works *by* the author

1. Titles. Alphabet the titles according to the basic rules for alphabetical arrangement as they may apply.

Example:
> Hawthorne, Nathaniel
>> The American notebooks.
>> Complete writings.
>> The scarlet letter.
>> Selected tales and sketches.
>> Twice-told tales.
>> Works.

2. Main and added entries. Interfile all main and added entries under the same author heading in one file. Subarrange alphabetically by the titles of the books. On added entries, disregard an author main entry, but alphabet by a title main entry. Examples follow 26B3 below.

3. Designations following heading. In both main and added entry headings disregard designations that show the relationship of the heading to one particular work, as "comp.," "ed.," "illus.," "tr.," "joint author [editor," etc.], "appellant," "defendant," etc.

Examples for 26B2–3:

> Pennell, Joseph, 1857–1926
> > The adventures of an illustrator.
>
> > Pennell, Joseph, 1857–1926, illus.
> Van Rennselaer, Mariana Griswold
> > English cathedrals . . .
>
> Pennell, Joseph, 1857–1926
> > Etchers and etching . . .
>
> > Pennell, Joseph, 1857–1926, joint author
> Pennell, Elizabeth Robins
> > The life of James McNeill Whistler.
>
> Pennell, Joseph, 1857–1926
> > Our journey to the Hebrides.

> American Society for Metals
> > Age hardening of metals.
>
> American Society for Metals
> French, Herbert James
> > Alloy construction steels.
>
> American Society for Metals
> > Atom movements.

> > Landsberg, Helmut, 1906–   ed.
> Advances in geophysics.
>
> Landsberg, Helmut, 1906–
> > Physical climatology.

4. Shorter title before longer. Arrange different titles that begin with the same words by the title proper, the shorter title before the longer, disregarding any subtitle, alternative title, "by" phrase, etc. that may follow the shorter title.

Examples:

> Auslander, Joseph
> > The winged horse; the story of the poets and their poetry.
> > The winged horse anthology.

Nelson, Oscar Severine
>   Accounting systems, by Oscar S. Nelson and Arthur D. Maxwell.
>   Accounting systems and data processing ₍by₎ Oscar S. Nelson ₍and₎ Richard S. Woods.

5. Author's name at beginning of title. At the beginning of a title the author's name, even in the possessive case, should be disregarded if it is simply an author statement transcribed from the work. However, if the name in the possessive case is the author's pseudonym, or if an author's name is an integral part of the title, do not disregard it in filing. Do not disregard a name other than the author's.

Examples:

Barlow, Peter
>   An essay on magnetic attraction.
>   <Barlow's> tables of squares, cubes, square roots . . .
>   A treatise on the strength of timber . . .

Shakespeare, William
>   Selections from Shakespeare.
>   The Shakespeare apocrypha.
>   Shakespeare's wit and humor.
>   Three tragedies.

Lawrence, Robert
>   Carmen.
>   Gilbert and Sullivan's H. M. S. Pinafore.
>   Gilbert and Sullivan's The Gondoliers.
>   Haensel and Gretel.

6. Translations. Arrange each translation alphabetically by its own title.

Example:

Mann, Thomas
>   Joseph in Egypt.
>   The magic mountain (Der Zauberberg)
>   A man and his dog.
>   La montagne magique (Der Zauberberg)

Young Joseph.
Der Zauberberg.

7. Editions published under different titles. Arrange each edition or issue of a work that is published under a different title alphabetically by its own title.

Example:

Maugham, W. Somerset
The circle.

Fools and their folly.
Originally published under title: Then and now.

The moon and sixpence.

Then and now.
Later published under title: Fools and their folly.

The trembling of a leaf.

8. Editions with the same title

cf. *Introductory notes* to this section, p. 33, Editions.

a. Basic rule. Arrange editions of all types of material that have the same title in straight chronological order by dates of publication, with earliest date first, disregarding any subtitles or edition numbers.

Example:

Briscoe, Herman Thompson
General chemistry for colleges. [c1935]
General chemistry for colleges. [c1938]
General chemistry for colleges. 3d ed. [1943]
General chemistry for colleges. 4th ed. [1949]

(1) When there are two or more entries with the same date, subarrange first alphabetically by place of publication, then by publisher, then by number of volumes, special edition, etc.

(2) Arrange dates according to the following example:

n. d.	193–?
1899	1930
19—?	1935
1900	1941 ⎫
1929	1941? ⎭ Interfile

b. **Variations in wording.** Slight variations in the wording of the title proper must be regarded. The presence of a subtitle, and variations in wording of subtitles, are disregarded, except when the subtitles show that the works are entirely different.

Examples:

Different main title:

Schultz, William John
 American public finance. 2d rev. ed. 1938.
  Previous editions have title: American public finance and taxation.

 American public finance. 3d ed. 1942.
 American public finance and taxation. 1931.
 American public finance and taxation. Rev. ed. 1934.
  Later edition has title: American public finance.

Subtitle disregarded:

Essipoff, Marie Armstrong
 Making the most of your food freezer; new ideas, new techniques, new recipes. ₁1951₁
 Making the most of your food freezer. ₁1954₁
 Making the most of your food freezer. Rev. and enl. by Edwina Jackson. ₁1961₁

Subtitle regarded:

Finney, Harry Anson
 Principles of accounting. 3d ed. 1946.
  Contents: ₁1₁ Intermediate. ₁2₁ Advanced.

 Principles of accounting. 4th ed. 1951–52.
 Principles of accounting. 5th ed. ₁1958₁–60.
 Principles of accounting, introductory. 3d ed. 1948.
 Principles of accounting, introductory. 4th ed. 1953.
 Principles of accounting, introductory. 5th ed. 1957.

c. **Abridged edition.** When everything else that is to be regarded is the same, file an abridged edition after the unabridged work.

Example:

Homer
    The Odyssey of Homer; translated by George Herbert
    Palmer. Boston, Houghton, Mifflin [c1891]
    The Odyssey of Homer; translated by George Herbert
    Palmer. Abridged school ed. Boston, Houghton, Mifflin
    [c1891]

If the imprint dates are different, the abridged edition is arranged in its chronological place by date.

Example:

Toynbee, Arnold Joseph
    A study of history. 1934–
    A study of history. Abridgement of volumes I–[X] by
  D. C. Somervell. 1947–57.
    A study of history. [1948]–61.

9. Author-title added entries. Arrange an author-title added entry by the title in the heading. If there are no main entries for the work in the catalog, file a secondary author-title heading in its alphabetical place, where the author-title main entries would be if there were any. If there are main entries for the work, arrange the author-title added entries after them, subarranged alphabetically by their main entries.

10. Analytical entries. Arrange an author analytic by the title of the analytic. If there are no main entries for the work in the catalog, file an author analytic in its alphabetical place, where the author-title main entries would be if there were any. If there is more than one such analytic, subarrange the entries chronologically by the imprint dates of the books. If there are main entries for the work, interfile analytics not made in the form of author-title added entries with them, subarranged chronologically by the imprint dates of the books. Arrange analytics made in the form of author-title added entries after main entries for the work, the analytics subarranged by their main entries.

11. Author-title subject entries. Arrange an author-title subject entry by the title in the heading. If there are no author entries for the work in the catalog, file an author-title subject entry in its alphabetical place, where the author entries would be if there were any. If there are author entries for the work, arrange author-title subject entries after them, subarranged alphabetically by their main entries.

12. Different kinds of entries for the same title. Arrange different kinds of entries for the same title under an author in groups in the following order:

1) Main entries for editions of the work as a separate and analytical entries that are not made in the form of an author-title added entry, interfiled and subarranged by imprint dates
2) Author-title added entries and author analytics made in the form of author-title added entries, interfiled and subarranged alphabetically by their main entries
3) Author-title subject entries, subarranged alphabetically by their main entries

Comprehensive examples for 26B8–12:

O'Neill, Eugene Gladstone

Anna Christie.
(In his The hairy ape, Anna Christie, The first man. [c1922])

"Anna Christie"; with twelve illus. by Alexander King. 1930.

Anna Christie.
(In Mantle, R. B. A treasury of the theatre. 1935)

Homer

The Odyssey of Homer. Translated by Alexander Pope. 1771.

Odyssey.
(In Chalmers, Alexander, ed. The works of the English poets. London, 1810)

Odyssey; done into English prose, by S. H. Butcher and A. Lang. Boston, Lothrop, 1882.

Odyssey; with introd., notes, etc. by W. W. Merry. 3d ed. Oxford, Clarendon Press, 1882–88. 2 v.

The Odyssey of Homer; translated by S. H. Butcher and

A. Lang; with introd., notes and illus. New York, Collier
[c1909] (The Harvard classics, v. 22) [analytic—unit card]
    The Odyssey of Homer, book XI.   Edited with introd.,
notes, vocabulary, and appendices by J. A. Nairn.   1924.
    The Odyssey of Homer, translated by George Herbert
Palmer, with illus. by N. C. Wyeth.   Cambridge, Hough-
ton, Mifflin, 1929.
    The Odyssey of Homer; translated into English verse
by Herbert Bates.   School ed.   New York, Harper, 1929.
    The Odyssey of Homer, done into English prose by S. H.
Butcher and A. Lang.   New York, Modern Library [1929]
    The Odyssey [by] Homer, including also passages from
Homer's Iliad, also Norse legends and American Indian
legends.   [1942]
    The Odyssey of Homer.   [c1951]
    The Odyssey.   Translated by Robert Fitzgerald.   With
drawings by Hans Erni.   [1963]

Homer
    The Odyssey.
Beny, Roloff
    A time of gods; a photographer in the wake of Odysseus.
    Quotations from Chapman's Homer . . .   [1962]

Homer
    The Odyssey.
Kazantzakēs, Nikos
    The odyssey; a modern sequel.   Translation into English
    verse . . . by Kimon Friar . . .   1958.

HOMER
    THE ODYSSEY.
Harrison, Jane Ellen
    Myths of the Odyssey in art and literature.

HOMER
    THE ODYSSEY.
Taylor, Charles Henry
    Essays on the Odyssey, selected modern criticism.

Homer
    The story of Odysseus.
    The toils and travels of Odysseus.

C. Works *about* **the author.** Arrange the subject entries for works *about* the author after all entries for works *by* the author, in two groups in the following order:

1) Subjects without subdivision, subarranged by their main entries, or if an analytic, by the entry for the analytic
   Exception: An author-title subject entry files in the author file in its alphabetical place by the title in the heading, immediately after the author entries for the same title if there are any (see Rule 26B11).

2) Subjects with subdivisions, arranged alphabetically by the subdivisions

Example:

Shakespeare, William, 1564–1616
    The winter's tale.

    SHAKESPEARE, WILLIAM, 1564–1616
Alexander, Peter
    Shakespeare.

    SHAKESPEARE, WILLIAM, 1564–1616
Brandes, Georg Morris Cohen
    William Shakespeare, a critical study.

SHAKESPEARE, WILLIAM, 1564–1616—BIBLIOGRAPHY
SHAKESPEARE, WILLIAM, 1564–1616—CHARACTERS
SHAKESPEARE, WILLIAM, 1564–1616, IN FICTION, DRAMA, POETRY, ETC.
SHAKESPEARE, WILLIAM, 1564–1616—NATURAL HISTORY

27. Organized author arrangement

For music uniform titles, see Rule 37B.

Preliminary note. This rule covers situations where the uniform title[5] system is applied in order to secure a special organized arrangement of titles, editions, and translations under an author. General guidelines for the establishment of uniform titles are provided in *Anglo-American Cataloging Rules* (Chapter 4). In the

---

5. Uniform title. The particular title by which a work that has appeared under varying titles is to be identified for cataloging purposes.

following example the form used in the cataloging rules is followed (i. e., uniform title in brackets added on line below author when the publication appears under a title different from that chosen for the uniform title).

General rules. Arrange uniform titles in their alphabetical places among other titles under an author entry. Arrange subheadings for parts and languages alphabetically, interfiled with each other, except numbered parts, which should be arranged numerically. Under a uniform title arrange the entries alphabetically by title page titles. When there are two or more entries with the same title page title, subarrange them by imprint dates, according to Rule 26B8.

Example:

Shakespeare, William, 1564–1616
    Aphorisms from Shakespeare
    see his Selections

    As you like it.

    Comedies, histories, & tragedies
    see his Works

    Doubtful plays
    see his Selected works

    Hamlet, edited for school use by William Allan Neilson.
1903.

    Hamlet.
    (In Gassner, J.   A treasury of the theatre.   ₍1951₎)

    Hamlet.   Additional notes and exercises by W. F. Langford.   ₍c1958₎

    ₍Hamlet₎
    Revealment of Hamlet, by Alfred Stoner.   ₍1952₎

    ₍Hamlet₎
    <Shakespeare's> tragedy of Hamlet, Prince of Denmark, edited, with notes, by William J. Rolfe.   ₍1903₎

    Shakespeare, William, 1564–1616   ₍analytic₎
      Hamlet.
Grebanier, Bernard D   N
    The heart of Hamlet: the play Shakespeare wrote, with

the text of the play as edited by Professor Grebanier.
[1960]

  Shakespeare, William, 1564–1616   [added entry]
  Hamlet.
MacKaye, Percy
  The mystery of Hamlet, King of Denmark; or, What we
  will, a tetralogy, in prologue to The tragical historie of
  Hamlet, Prince of Denmarke, by William Shakespeare.
  1950.

  SHAKESPEARE, WILLIAM, 1564–1616
  HAMLET.
Leavenworth, Russell E
  Interpreting Hamlet.

Shakespeare, William, 1564–1616
  [Hamlet. French]
  La tragique histoire de Hamlet prince de Danemark, tr.
  par Guy de Pourtalès . . . 1923.

  Henry IV   [same for V, VI, VIII]
  see his King Henry IV

  Julius Caesar. A midsummer-night's dream.   [1942]
  King Henry IV.[6]
  King Henry IV. Part I.
  King Henry IV. Part II.
  King Henry V.

  Locrine
  see Locrine (Old play)

  [Lucrece]
  <Shakespeare's> Rape of Lucrece; with preface, glossary, &c. by Israel Gollancz. 1904.

  Plays
  see his Selected works
        Works

---

6. Arrange all kings in chronological order.

Shakespeare, William, 1564–1616   ₁note card₁
   Poems.
     Included under this title are collections and selections
of the poems, including songs.
     For the Sonnets alone, and for single poems, see the
specific title, e. g.,
   Sonnets
   Lucrece

   <Shakespeare's> poems: Venus and Adonis, Lucrece,
Sonnets, etc. Edited, with notes, by William J. Rolfe. 1890.

   ₁Poems₁
   Songs and sonnets. Edited by F. T. Palgrave. 1879.

   Rape of Lucrece
   see his Lucrece

   Revealment of Hamlet
   see his Hamlet

   The riddle of Shakespeare's sonnets
   see his Sonnets

Shakespeare, William, 1564–1616   ₁note card₁
   Selected works.
     Included under this title are partial collections of
whole works.

   ₁Selected works₁
   Doubtful plays of William Shakespeare . . . 1869.

   ₁Selected works₁
   Hamlet, Prince of Denmark, The tempest, The tragedy
of King Richard the Second. ₁c1932₁

   ₁Selected works₁
   Plays of Shakespeare, selected and prepared for use in
schools, clubs, classes, and families . . . 1880.

   ₁Selected works₁
   <Shakespeare's> tragedies. ₁1906₁

Shakespeare, William, 1564–1616   ₁note card₁
   Selections.
     Included under this title are collections consisting of
parts of various works, extracts, quotations, etc.

⌐Selections⌐
Aphorisms from Shakespeare . . .   1812.

Selections from Shakspeare.   By Benjamin Oakley.
1828.

⌐Selections⌐
Shakespeare's wit and humour, by William A. Lawson.
⌐1912⌐

⌐Selections⌐
The Shakespearian dictionary . . .   1832.

Shakespeare, William, 1564–1616
Smith, Charles George
Shakespeare's proverb lore; his use of the Sententiae of
Leonard Culman and Publilius Syrus.   1963.

The Shakespearian dictionary
see his Selections

Songs
see his Poems

⌐Sonnets⌐
The riddle of Shakespeare's sonnets: the text of the sonnets, with interpretive essays by Edward Hubler . . .
⌐1962⌐

The sonnets of Shakespeare and Milton.   1830.

Tragedies
see his Selected works

Tragedy of Hamlet
see his Hamlet

The two noble kinsmen
see Fletcher, John
    The two noble kinsmen

Venus and Adonis.
<Shakespeare's> will . . .   1851.

Shakespeare, William, 1564–1616   ⌐note card⌐
    Works.
        Included under this title are complete works, includ-
ing complete dramatic works.

[Works]

<Mr. William Shakespeare's> comedies, histories, and tragedies, faithfully reproduced in facsimile from the edition of 1685. 1904.

[Works]

A new variorum edition of Shakespeare, edited by Horace Howard Furness. 1871–19

[Works]

<Shakespeare's> plays; with his life . . . Ed. by Gulian C. Verplanck . . . 1847.

The works of Shakespeare, edited by Israel Gollancz. 1899–1900.

[Works. Spanish]
Dramas. [1933]

[Works. Spanish]
Obras dramáticas. 1887–99.

SHAKESPEARE, WILLIAM, 1564–1616—BIBLIOGRAPHY
SHAKESPEARE, WILLIAM, 1564–1616—COMEDIES

28. Corporate entry arrangement

For corporate entries beginning with a geographical name, see Rule 31.

For special forms of corporate entries that begin with a surname, see Rule 23.

A. Filing position. Arrange corporate entries in their alphabetical places like titles.

Example:

American leaders in world affairs	[title]
American Library Association	[corporate heading]
American life in the eighties	[title]

B. Different kinds of entries under same name. Arrange different kinds of entries under the same corporate name in groups in the following order:

1) Author (main and/or added entry) without subheading, subarranged by titles according to Rule 26
2) Subject without subdivision, and identical title added

47

entries, interfiled and subarranged alphabetically by
their main entries

3) Name with corporate and/or subject subdivisions, the
subdivisions interfiled alphabetically with each other and
with titles, longer corporate names beginning with the
same words, etc., disregarding punctuation; each corporate author heading followed by its own subject entries.
Arrange headings for committees, departments, offices,
etc. by the first word of the subheading (see Rule 31D).

Examples:

National Research Council
National Research Council. Building Research Advisory
      Board
National Research Council. Building Research Institute
National Research Council (Canada)
National Research Council (Canada)   Division of Building
      Research
National Research Council (Canada)   Technical Information
      Service
National Research Council. Committee on Nuclear Science
National Research Council Conference on Glossary of Terms
      in Nuclear Science and Technology
National Research Council. Disaster Research
National Research Council. Nuclear Science Committee, *see*
      National Research Council. Committee on Nuclear
      Science
National Research Council of Canada, *see* National Research
      Council (Canada)
National Research Council of the Philippine Islands
National Research Council. Office of Critical Tables

United Nations   ₍author entries₎
UNITED NATIONS
United Nations and how it works
UNITED NATIONS—BIOGRAPHY
United Nations. Charter
United Nations. Economic Commission for Europe
United Nations Educational, Scientific and Cultural
      Organization

UNITED NATIONS—EGYPT
UNITED NATIONS EMERGENCY FORCE
United Nations forces   ⌜title⌝
UNITED NATIONS—YEARBOOKS

ANONYMOUS CLASSIC ENTRY
ARRANGEMENT
(RULES 29–30)

29. Bible

Note. The rules for Bible headings in the *Anglo-American
Cataloging Rules* are different in several respects from previous cataloging rules. There will be fewer entries under
Bible than formerly, some of the entries under Bible will be
simpler, and some of the changes will have a major effect on
the arrangement of Bible entries in the catalog. In all areas
of change the new entry rules result in a more desirable filing
order. The changes that will have the most widespread effect
are:

1) *Versions.* Name of version will precede date in the
heading.

2) *Selections.* The subheading "Selections" will follow
language and version in the heading.

A. Filing position. Entries for Bible, the sacred book, follow
entries for the single surname Bible.

B. Basic order. Arrange Bible entries in straight alphabetical
order word by word, disregarding kind of entry, form of heading,
and punctuation.[7] Under the same author heading subarrange
alphabetically by titles.

---

7. Libraries that prefer grouped arrangements for the Bible and its parts
may find rules for such arrangements in American Library Association.
A. L. A. Rules for Filing Catalog Cards. Chicago, 1942, and U. S. Library
of Congress. Processing Dept. *Filing Rules for the Dictionary Catalogs of the
Library of Congress.* Washington, 1956.

C. Dates in headings. Arrange headings which include a date alphabetically up to the date, then arrange the same headings with different dates chronologically by date, earliest date first. For details of date arrangement follow Rule 26B8a(2).

Old- and new-form headings that are the same except for order of the elements may be interfiled and arranged in the position of the new headings, with the key word in the old-form headings indicated in some way.

Example:

Bible. English. 1912
Bible. English. Authorized. 1854
Bible. English. 1943. <u>A</u>uthorized   [old form]
Bible. English. Authorized. 1962
Bible. English.↑ Selections. 1941. <u>A</u>uthorized   [old form]
Bible. English. Authorized. <u>Selections</u>. 1958

D. Different kinds of entries under the same heading. Arrange different kinds of entries under the same heading in groups in the following order:

1) Author (main and/or added entry), subarranged alphabetically by titles according to Rule 26
2) Subject, subarranged alphabetically by main entries

E. Parts of books. Arrange entries for chapters and verses after all entries for the whole book, in numerical order. The larger part beginning with the same chapter precedes the smaller part. Verses under the same chapter are arranged numerically by the first number.

Example:

Bible. N. T. Luke. English. 1960
Bible. N. T. Luke I–LI
           I–II
           I, 5–II, 40
           I, 26–38, II, 1–20
           II, 1–20

F. Numbered books. Numbered books of the Bible follow in numerical order the same name used collectively without number. Arrange in the following order:

1) Headings for the whole, with all its author and subject subdivisions alphabetically
2) Headings for numbered books, in numerical order, each arranged in two groups as follows:
    a) alphabetical—for author and subject subdivisions
    b) numerical—for chapters and verses

Example:

BIBLE. N. T. CORINTHIANS—COMMENTARIES
Bible. N. T. Corinthians. English. 1961
BIBLE. N. T. 1 CORINTHIANS—COMMENTARIES
Bible. N. T. 1 Corinthians. English. 1958
BIBLE. N. T. 1 CORINTHIANS X–XI—
COMMENTARIES
BIBLE. N. T. 2 CORINTHIANS—COMMENTARIES

G. Abbreviations. Arrange the abbreviations "N. T." and "O. T." used when followed by a subheading, as "New Testament" and "Old Testament."

Comprehensive example for Rule 29:[8]

Bible, Danà Xenophon
Bible   [author entries]
BIBLE
Bible. Acts, *see* Bible N. T. Acts
BIBLE AND SCIENCE
BIBLE—ANTIQUITIES
Bible. Apocrypha, *see* Bible. O. T. Apocrypha
Bible biographies
BIBLE—BIOGRAPHY
Bible. English. 1875
Bible. English. 1912
Bible. English. American Revised. 1966
Bible. English. Authorized. 193–?
    The Holy Bible containing the Old and New Testaments . . .
Bible. English. Authorized. 193–?
    The Oxford self-pronouncing Bible.

---

8. All examples are shown in the new form according to the *Anglo-American Cataloging Rules.*

Bible. English. Authorized. 1930
Bible. English. Authorized. 1949
Bible. English. Authorized. Selections. 1941
Bible. English. Authorized. Selections. 1958
Bible. English (Basic English) 1949
BIBLE. ENGLISH—BIBLIOGRAPHY
BIBLE. ENGLISH—HISTORY
Bible. English. Revised. 1923
Bible. English. Revised standard. 1956
Bible. English. Selections. 1925
BIBLE. ENGLISH—VERSIONS
Bible. Epistle of Barnabas, *see* Epistle of Barnabas
Bible. Greek. Codex Sinaiticus
The Bible in art
BIBLE IN LITERATURE
BIBLE—MANUSCRIPTS
BIBLE—MANUSCRIPTS, ANGLO–SAXON
BIBLE. N. T. ACTS—BIOGRAPHY
Bible. N. T. Acts. English. Authorized. 1959
Bible. N. T. Acts. English. Barclay. 1957
BIBLE. N. T.—COMMENTARIES
Bible. N. T. English. American revised. 1959
Bible. N. T. Epistle of Barnabas, *see* Epistle of Barnabas
Bible. N. T. Epistles. English. Phillips. 1957
Bible. N. T. Epistles of John. English. Barclay. 1960
Bible. N. T. Philippians
The Bible of the world
Bible. O. T. [same arrangement as N. T.]
BIBLE—PARAPHRASES
Bible. Philippians, *see* Bible. N. T. Philippians
Bible. Polyglot. 1957
BIBLE STORIES
Bible. Welsh . . .

30. Other anonymous classics and sacred books

A. General rule. Arrange sacred scriptures other than the Bible
in the same manner as Bible entries, in straight alphabetical order
word by word (see Rule 29).

Under the same heading arrange all entries according to the
regular rules for author arrangement (Rule 26).

Example:

Talmud, Ėra Davidovna
Talmud
TALMUD
Talmud. Baba batra
TALMUD. BABA BATRA—COMMENTARIES
Talmud. Baba batra. Hebrew
Talmud. Baba batra. Selections
TALMUD—COMMENTARIES
Talmud. English
Talmud. English. Selections
Talmud. Minor tractates
Talmud. Selections
The Talmud unmasked
Talmud Yerushalmi
Talmud. Yiddish

B. Anonymous classic with explanatory designation in parentheses. Arrange an anonymous classic heading that consists of one or more words or a personal name followed by an explanatory designation in parentheses in its alphabetical place with other kinds of entries. Disregard the parentheses and alphabet by the word or words enclosed therein.

Example:

Genesis   [title of a book]
Genesis and birth of the Federal Constitution
Genesis and Exodus (Middle English poem)
Genesis and modern science
Genesis (Anglo–Saxon poem)
Genesis (Book of the Old Testament) *see* . . .
Genesis Down   [fiction title]

31. Place arrangement

A. Filing position. Entries beginning with a geographical name follow the same name used as a single surname.

B. Basic order. Arrange all entries beginning with the same geographical name in one straight alphabetical file, word by word, disregarding punctuation.

For details of arrangement of subject subdivisions under place, see Rule 32.

C. Different kinds of entries under the same heading. Arrange different kinds of entries under the same geographical name heading in groups in the following order:

1) Author (main and/or added entry) without subheading, subarranged by titles according to Rule 26. Disregard terms such as "appellant," "defendant," etc., which show the relationship of the place to one particular work, and alphabet by the title.

2) Subject without subdivision, and identical title added entries, interfiled and subarranged alphabetically by their main entries

3) Heading with corporate and/or subject subdivisions, the subdivisions interfiled alphabetically with each other and with titles, etc., disregarding punctuation; each corporate author heading followed by its own subject entries

D. Official governmental divisions. Arrange headings for the official governmental divisions of a place (i.e., bureaus, committees, departments, etc.) by the first word of the subheading, e. g.,

U. S.   Bureau of Education
U. S.   Dept. of Agriculture

with a reference from the distinctive word in the subheading, e. g.,

U. S.   Agriculture, Dept. of, *see* U. S.   Dept. of Agriculture

E. Different places of the same name. Different places, jurisdictions, and governments of the same name are alphabeted by the geographical or parenthetical designations following the names. Arrangement is first by the complete designation, then under each different heading according to the general rules 31B-D above.

Examples for Rule 31:

United States
UNITED STATES
U. S.   Adjutant–General's Office
U. S.   ADJUTANT–GENERAL'S OFFICE
U. S.   Agricultural Adjustment Administration
United States Agricultural Society
U. S.—AGRICULTURE, *see* AGRICULTURE—U. S.

U. S. Agriculture, Dept. of, *see* U. S. Dept. of Agriculture
The United States among the nations   ₍title₎
U. S. Bureau of Education
U. S. Bureau of Standards, *see* U. S. National Bureau of
     Standards
U. S. camera
UNITED STATES (FRIGATE)
U. S. Government research reports   ₍title₎
U. S. National Bureau of Standards
U. S. Office of Education
U. S. Standards, Bureau of, *see* U. S. National Bureau of
     Standards
United States Steel Corporation
U. S.—TERRITORIAL EXPANSION

Each city with geographical designation:

Lincoln, William Sever
Lincoln and Ann Rutledge
LINCOLN, BATTLE OF, 1217
LINCOLN CO., KY.
Lincoln, Eng.
LINCOLN HIGHWAY
Lincoln, Neb.
LINCOLN, NEB.—BIOGRAPHY
Lincoln, Neb. Charter
Lincoln plays   ₍title₎

Each jurisdiction with designation:

New York Academy of Medicine
New York and the Seabury investigation   ₍title₎
New York (Archdiocese)
NEW YORK (BATTLESHIP)
New York Business Development Corporation
New York (City)
New York (City) Board of Education
NEW YORK (CITY)—CHARITIES
New York City Council of Political Reform
NEW YORK (CITY)—DESCRIPTION

New York City folklore   [title]
New York (City)   Public Library, *see* New York Public
    Library
New York cookbook   [title]
New York (County)
NEW YORK METROPOLITAN AREA
New York Public Library
New York (State)
New York (State)   Agricultural Experiment Station, Ithaca
New York State Bar Association
NEW YORK (STATE)—HISTORY
New York (State)   State College for Teachers, Albany
New York University

Chief city without geographical designation:

London, Jack
London   [place as author]
LONDON
London and Londoners   [title]
London. Central Criminal Court
LONDON, DECLARATION OF, 1909
LONDON—DESCRIPTION
London (Diocese)
LONDON (DOG)
LONDON IN LITERATURE
London, Ky.
London. National Gallery
London, Ont. Council
LONDON, ONT.—HISTORY
London scene   [title]
LONDON—WHARVES

State, without designation; including cities of same name and
institution with subdivisions:

California
California. Adjutant General's Office
California as I saw it   [title]
CALIFORNIA, GULF OF

California Institute of Technology, Pasadena
California. Legislature
California, Mo.
CALIFORNIA—POLITICS AND GOVERNMENT
California (Province)
California. Secretary of State
CALIFORNIA, SOUTHERN
CALIFORNIA, SOUTHERN—CLIMATE
California State Chamber of Commerce
California. University
California. University. Art Dept.
California. University at Los Angeles, *see* California. University. University at Los Angeles
CALIFORNIA. UNIVERSITY—BIOGRAPHY
California. University, Davis
California. University. Library
California. University. School of Law
California. University. University at Los Angeles
California. University. University at Los Angeles. Bureau of Governmental Research
California. University. University Extension
California. Vocational Rehabilitation Service

Country with parenthetical designations:

GERMANY—BIBLIOGRAPHY
Germany. Constitution
Germany (Democratic Republic)
GERMANY (DEMOCRATIC REPUBLIC)
Germany (Democratic Republic) Constitution
GERMANY (DEMOCRATIC REPUBLIC)—ECONOMIC CONDITIONS
GERMANY—DESCRIPTION AND TRAVEL
Germany divided   [title]
GERMANY, EASTERN
Germany (Federal Republic)
Germany plots with the Kremlin   [title]
Germany (Territory under Allied occupation, 1945–1955)
GERMANY (TERRITORY UNDER ALLIED OCCUPATION, 1945–1955)—POLITICS AND GOVERNMENT

57

Germany (Territory under Allied occupation, 1945–1955.
British Zone)

32. Subject arrangement

A. Filing position. Subject entries follow the same word used as
a single surname.

B. Identical subject entries—Subarrangement. Arrange entries
with the same subject heading alphabetically by their main entries,
then by title. Arrange subject analytics by the entry for the analytic
if different from the main entry for the whole book.

Example:

BISON, AMERICAN
Allen, Joel Asaph
    The American bisons, living and extinct.

BISON, AMERICAN
Anderson, George S
    A buffalo story.
    (In Roosevelt, Theodore.   American big-game hunting)

BISON, AMERICAN
Garretson, Martin S
    The American bison.

BISON, AMERICAN
Garretson, Martin S
    A short history of the American bison.

C. Basic order. Arrange a subject, its subdivisions, etc., in
groups in the following order:
1) Subject without subdivision, interfiled with identical title
   added entries alphabetically by their main entries
2) Period divisions, arranged chronologically (for detailed
   rules see 32E below)
3) Alphabetical extensions of the main subject heading:
   form, subject, and geographical subdivisions, inverted subject headings, subject followed by a parenthetical term,
   and phrase subject headings, interfiled word by word in
   one alphabet with titles and other headings beginning
   with the same word, disregarding punctuation

D. Further subdivisions. Arrange the further subdivisions of subheadings in the same order as the subheadings themselves are arranged (according to 32C above).

E. Period divisions

1. Arrange period divisions chronologically by the first date in the heading.

Periods of time beginning with the same year but extending to different years are arranged so as to bring the longest period first. If a period subdivision is open (e. g., 1865–   ), it precedes all other period subdivisions beginning with the same or later years.

2. Period divisions in the form of phrases (e. g., U. S.—HISTORY—COLONIAL PERIOD) and those consisting of a distinctive word, name, or phrase followed by dates (e. g., GT. BRIT.—HISTORY—RESTORATION, 1660–1688) are arranged chronologically, not alphabetically.

3. Under language and literature subjects, such subdivisions as OLD FRENCH; EARLY MODERN (TO 1700); 18TH CENTURY, etc., are regarded as period subvidisions.

4. The divisions ANCIENT, MEDIEVAL, MODERN, etc. are arranged alphabetically, not chronologically, even when followed by a date (e. g., HISTORY, MODERN—20TH CENTURY), except when used as further divisions of the subdivisions HISTORY or HISTORY AND CRITICISM (e. g., MUSIC—HISTORY AND CRITICISM—ANCIENT).

Examples for Rule 32:

GENERAL EXAMPLES OF ORDER—
WITHOUT ANY PERIOD SUBDIVISIONS

COOKERY
COOKERY, AMERICAN
COOKERY, AMERICAN—ALASKA
COOKERY, AMERICAN—BIBLIOGRAPHY
COOKERY, AMERICAN—CALIFORNIA
COOKERY (APPLES)
COOKERY, CHINESE
COOKERY—DICTIONARIES
COOKERY FOR DIABETICS
Cookery for girls   [title]
COOKERY, INTERNATIONAL
COOKERY—YEARBOOKS

Parenthetical term indicating different aspects and/or different subjects, not used with one of the headings:

MASS
Mass and Lord's prayer   ₍title₎
MASS—CELEBRATION
MASS COMMUNICATION
MASS (MUSIC)
Mass of the Roman rite   ₍title₎
MASS (PHYSICS)
MASS—STUDY AND TEACHING

GENERAL EXAMPLES OF ORDER—
WITH PERIOD SUBDIVISIONS

EDUCATION
EDUCATION—1945–
EDUCATION—1945–   ADDRESSES, ESSAYS, LEC-
    TURES
EDUCATION—AFRICA
EDUCATION—AIMS AND OBJECTIVES
EDUCATION, ANCIENT
Education and American civilization   ₍title₎
EDUCATION—COLLECTIONS
EDUCATION, MEDIEVAL
EDUCATION OF CHILDREN
Education through art   ₍title₎
EDUCATION—U. S.
EDUCATION—U. S.—1945–
EDUCATION—U. S.—1945–   ADDRESSES, ESSAYS,
    LECTURES
EDUCATION—U. S.—BIBLIOGRAPHY
EDUCATION—YEARBOOKS

Details of period divisions:

U. S.—HISTORY
            —COLONIAL PERIOD   ₍chronological
                                        group₎

                —KING WILLIAM'S WAR, 1689–1697
                —FRENCH AND INDIAN WAR, 1755–
                    1763
                —REVOLUTION
                —REVOLUTION—CAMPAIGNS AND
                    BATTLES
                —REVOLUTION—SOURCES
                —1783–1865
                —CONFEDERATION, 1783–1789
                —1801–1809
                —WAR OF 1812
                —1849–1877
                —CIVIL WAR
                —1865–
                —1865–1898
                —1898–
                —WAR OF 1898
                —20TH CENTURY
                —1933–1945
U. S.—HISTORY—BIBLIOGRAPHY   ₍alphabetical group₎
U. S. history bonus book   ₍title₎
U. S.—HISTORY, MILITARY
U. S.—HISTORY—SOURCES

ROME—HISTORY—REPUBLIC, 510–30 B. C.
                —REPUBLIC, 510–265 B. C.
                —EMPIRE, 30 B. C.–476 A. D.
                —TIBERIUS, 14–37

Literature headings:

ENGLISH LITERATURE
                        ₍chronological group₎
                —OLD ENGLISH, *see* ANGLO-
                    SAXON LITERATURE
                —MIDDLE ENGLISH (1100–
                    1500)
                —MIDDLE ENGLISH (1100–
                    1500)—HISTORY AND
                    CRITICISM
                —EARLY MODERN (TO 1700)
                —18TH CENTURY

61

ENGLISH LITERATURE—ADDRESSES, ESSAYS,
　　LECTURES　　　　　　　　　　[alphabetical group]
English literature and the Hebrew renaissance　　　　[title]
ENGLISH LITERATURE—AUSTRALIA, *see* AUSTRAL-
　　IAN LITERATURE
ENGLISH LITERATURE—CATHOLIC AUTHORS
ENGLISH LITERATURE (COLLECTIONS)
ENGLISH LITERATURE—HISTORY AND CRITICISM

Ancient, Medieval, Modern, etc.:

HISTORY
HISTORY, ANCIENT
History and evolution of Freemasonry　　　　　　　[title]
HISTORY—DICTIONARIES
HISTORY, MEDIEVAL, *see* . . .
HISTORY—METHODOLOGY
HISTORY, MODERN
HISTORY, MODERN—1945–

Dates denoting different things:

RECONSTRUCTION
RECONSTRUCTION—BIBLIOGRAPHY
Reconstruction Finance Corporation
RECONSTRUCTION—MISSISSIPPI
RECONSTRUCTION (1914–1939)
RECONSTRUCTION (1914–1939)—EUROPE
RECONSTRUCTION (1939–1951)

33. Title entry arrangement

Preliminary note. This rule covers title added entries and title
main entries.

A. Filing position. Arrange title entries in their alphabetical
places with other kinds of entries, after surname entries under the
same word. Follow the basic rules for alphabetical arrangement as
they may apply (e. g., disregard initial articles).

B. Identical title added entries—Subarrangement

1. Arrange identical title added entries alphabetically by their main entries. Arrange title analytics by the entry for the analytic if different from the main entry for the whole book.

Example:

> Electra
> Euripides
>
> Electra
> Giraudoux, Jean
> > (In Bentley, E. R. The modern theatre. 1955. v. 1)
>
> Electra
> Sophocles

2. Arrange different editions of the same title chronologically by their imprint dates, following the same rules as those for arrangement under author (Rule 26B8).

C. Order of title main entries, title added entries, and other kinds of entries under the same word or words. Arrange title main and added entries and other kinds of entries under the same word or words in groups in the following order (all examples follow 33D below):

1) Personal name or pseudonym; corporate name, place name, or uniform title heading

2) Subject *see* reference

3) Title entries for periodicals and newspapers (for details of subarrangement see 33D below)

4) Title *main* entries for separate works and serials other than periodicals and newspapers, subarranged in groups in the following order:

a) Those with nothing following the title, subarranged by place of publication

b) Those with subtitles or other phrases following the title, subarranged alphabetically by the subtitles or phrases

In relation to other entries in the catalog consider only the title proper. Regard a subtitle only when there is more than one entry with the same main title, to distinguish between them.

5) Title *added* entries (titles with authors) and identical subject entries, interfiled and subarranged alphabetically by their main entries

6) Longer entries beginning with the same word or words

D. Title main entries for periodicals and newspapers—Details . of subarrangement

1. In title main entries for periodicals and newspapers disregard subtitles and alternative titles. In relation to other entries in the catalog consider only the title proper. Subarrange identical titles first by place of publication and then by date, with earliest date first.

2. Arrange different kinds of entries under the title of the same publication in groups in the following order:

1) Title main entry for the publication

2) Author entries (main and/or added entries) for the publication, subarranged alphabetically by titles according to Rule 26B2

   Note. Periodical and newspaper titles will no longer be used as author main entries; they will be used as added entries instead *(Anglo-American Cataloging Rules)*. The filing order will be the same whether the heading is a main entry or an added entry.

3) Subject entries for the publication, subarranged by their main entries

3. In author and subject headings for a periodical or newspaper disregard a place of publication following the title in relation to other entries in the catalog. Regard it only when there are entries for more than one serial with the same title, to distinguish between them.

Arrange the author and subject headings for each different publication following the corresponding title main entry (or in the position of the title itself if there is no entry for it).

Examples for 33C–D:

Abraham Lincoln.   New York, Gilbertson Co., 1958.

Abraham Lincoln.   ₍South Pasadena, Calif., W. A. Abbott, c1919₎

Abraham Lincoln: an appreciation.   New York, Francis D.
   Tandy Co. [1906]
Abraham Lincoln.   By an Oxford M. A.   Portsmouth [Eng.]
   Holbrook & Son [1920?]
Abraham Lincoln: the story of his life . . .   [Boston, Boston
   Sunday Globe, 1909]

   Abraham Lincoln
Drinkwater, John

Abraham Lincoln Association, Springfield, Ill.

ECONOMIC GEOLOGY, *see* . . .
Economic geology.   v. 1–   Oct. 1905–   Lancaster, Pa.
   [etc.]

Life, Cora Smith
Life.   v. 1–   Nov. 23, 1936–   Chicago.

   Life (Chicago)
Boswell, Peyton
   Modern American painting.

Life (Chicago)
   The world's great religions.
LIFE (CHICAGO)
Life.   v. 1–103; 1883–Nov. 1936.   New York.

   Life (New York)
The Spice of Life.

Life (New York)
   War as viewed by Life.
The life.   Boston, Colby & Rich [187–?]   [title main entry]

   LIFE
Mayer, Charles Leopold

   Life
Rutherford, Joseph Franklin

   LIFE
St. John-Stevas, Norman

Life can begin again
LIFE—ORIGIN

United Nations   [author entry]
The United Nations (Periodical) *see* . . .
UNITED NATIONS
United Nations.   Charter

"Who's who," a directory of Stratford.   [1st–   1937–
Who's who . . . an annual biographical dictionary . . .   18   –
Who's who; the official who's who among students in American
    universities and colleges.   v. 1–   1935–

Who's who
Columbus, Ohio.   Chamber of Commerce

Who's who in America; a biographical dictionary of notable
    living men and women.   v. [1]–   1899–1900—

34. Series entry arrangement

A. Series entries under title. Arrange series entries and series
references under title in their alphabetical places with other titles,
etc. Arrange a series entry after an identical *see* reference.

1. Unnumbered series. Subarrange unnumbered series entries
alphabetically by their main entries.

Example:

Our debt to Greece and Rome   [series]
Nixon, Paul
    Martial and the modern epigram.

Our debt to Greece and Rome   [title added entry]
Osborn, Edward Bolland

Our debt to Greece and Rome   [series]
Roberts, William Rhys
    Greek rhetoric and literary criticism.

2. Numbered series. Subarrange numbered series numerically.

Examples:

The Reference shelf, v. 35, no. 6
Steel, Ronald
    Italy.

The Reference shelf, v. 36, no. 1
Colby, Vineta
American culture in the sixties.

The Reference shelf, v. 36, no. 2
Madow, Pauline
The Peace Corps.

AMERICAN STATESMEN, *see* . . .

American statesmen, v. 1
Morse, John Torrey
Benjamin Franklin.

American statesmen, v. 31
McCall, Samuel Walker
Thaddeus Stevens.

American statesmen. Second series, v. 2
Burton, Theodore Elijah
John Sherman.

American statesmen   ₍title added entry₎
Griggs, Edward Howard

3. Dated series. Subarrange dated series chronologically.

Example:

The Charles Eliot Norton lectures, 1937–1938
Tinker, Chauncey Brewster
Painter and poet.

The Charles Eliot Norton lectures, 1953–1954
Read, Sir Herbert Edward
Icon and idea.

B. Series entries under author and title
1. Arrange author-title series entries and series references alphabetically the same as any author-title entry, interfiling the series titles with other titles that have the same author entry.
2. Subarrange author-title series the same as series under title, i. e., alphabetically by main entry, numerically, or chronologically, depending on the form of the heading.

Example for 34B:

    American Management Association
      Reporting sales data effectively.

    American Management Association
      Research report, no. 6.
  Dale, Ernest
    The unionization of foremen.

    American Management Association
      Research report, no. 18.
  Cutter, Walter Airey
    Organization and functions of the safety department.

American Management Association
  The sales supervisor and his place in management.

35. Cross reference arrangement

A. Filing position. A reference or explanatory note precedes all other entries under the same word or words. In relation to other entries in the catalog consider only the heading on a cross reference or explanatory note; disregard the words "see" and "see also," the heading or headings referred to, and the note.

B. "See" references

1. File *see* references in their alphabetical places. *See* references from subject subdivisions, inverted subjects, etc. are arranged according to the regular rules for subject arrangement.

Examples:

  Henry, Norman Fordyce McKerron
  Henry, O., *see* Porter, William Sydney
  Henry, Omer

  The county fair
  COUNTY FINANCE, *see* . . .
  COUNTY GOVERNMENT

  HYGIENE
  HYGIENE, DENTAL, *see* . . .
  Hygiene for students
  HYGIENE—HISTORY

MOVING-PICTURES
MOVING-PICTURES—CENSORSHIP
MOVING-PICTURES—COPYRIGHT, *see* . . .
MOVING-PICTURES, DOCUMENTARY

2. If a *see* reference is the same as an actual entry, arrange the *see* reference first, except that a surname entry always precedes a reference.

Examples:

Corea, Lois Fleming
 New marine mollusks.
COREA, *see* KOREA

DOCTORS, *see* PHYSICIANS

 The doctors   [fiction title]
Soubiran, André

C. "See also" references. File a *see also* reference before the first entry under the same word or words. If *see also* references are made for headings under which there are no entries in the catalog, file the reference where the heading itself would be filed.

Examples:

CHILDREN, *see also* . . .
CHILDREN
CHILDREN—CARE AND HYGIENE, *see also* . . .
CHILDREN—CARE AND HYGIENE
CHILDREN—CARE AND HYGIENE—BIBLIOGRAPHY

TREASON, *see also* . . .

 Treason   [fiction title]
Gessner, Robert

 TREASON
Thérive, André

Treason at the point
TREASON—CANADA

D. Author-title references. Arrange author-title references (which may be used for certain pseudonyms, series, legal headings, uniform titles, etc.) in their alphabetical places as if they were author and title entries.

Examples:
> United States
>> Chamizal arbitration.
> United States
>> Constitution
>> *see* U. S. Constitution
> United States
>> The counter case of the United States of America . . .

E. Explanatory cards. File explanatory notes and references before the first entry under the same heading.

Examples:
> Epstein, Beryl Williams
>> Works by Beryl Williams Epstein in collaboration with Samuel Epstein, published under the names Adam Allen and Douglas Coe, are entered in this catalog under Allen, Adam and Coe, Douglas, respectively.
> Epstein, Beryl Williams
>> Fashion is our business.

> INTERPLANETARY VOYAGES
>> Here are entered the early, imaginary, and descriptive accounts of travel beyond the earth.
>> Works on the physics and technical details of flight beyond the atmosphere of the earth are entered under the heading SPACE FLIGHT.
> INTERPLANETARY VOYAGES, *see also* . . .

> INTERPLANETARY VOYAGES
> Coggins, Jack
>> By space ship to the moon.

36. Numerical and chronological arrangement

A. General rule. A numerical or a chronological arrangement, rather than an alphabetical, should be followed when numbers or dates distinguish between entries, or headings, otherwise identical, with lowest number or earliest date first.

In relation to other entries in the catalog disregard a numeral or date that indicates a sequence. Regard it only for the purpose of arranging a sequence. If the number precedes the item it modifies it must be mentally transposed to follow the item (i. e., file "U. S. Army. 1st Cavalry" as "U. S. Army. Cavalry, 1st").

B. Titles

Numerical designations following or at end of titles that are otherwise identical up to that point

Examples:

More, Paul Elmer
    Aristocracy and justice; Shelburne essays, ninth series.
More, Paul Elmer
    Pages from an Oxford diary.
More, Paul Elmer
    Shelburne essays.   1st series.
More, Paul Elmer
    Shelburne essays.   Second series.
More, Paul Elmer
    Shelburne essays.   Fourth series.
More, Paul Elmer
    Shelburne essays.   Ninth series
    see his Aristocracy and justice

Bolles, Albert Sidney
    The financial history of the United States, from 1774 to 1789.
    The financial history of the United States, from 1789 to 1860.

C. Corporate headings—General examples

1. Dates only

Example:

Massachusetts.   Constitutional Convention, 1779–1780
Massachusetts.   Constitutional Convention, 1853

2. Number only

Examples:

Lexington (U. S. aircraft carrier, 1st of the name)
Lexington (U. S. aircraft carrier, 2d of the name)

U. S. Circuit Court (1st Circuit)
U. S. Circuit Court (5th Circuit)

3. Number and date. Disregard a place name when it follows a number.

Example:

American Peace Congress, 1st, New York, 1907
American Peace Congress, 3d, Baltimore, 1911
American Peace Congress, 4th, St. Louis, 1913

4. Place and date. If there is no numeral to indicate a sequence, the heading being followed only by a place and date in that order, arrange alphabetically by the place, disregarding the date at end.

Example:

OLYMPIC GAMES
Olympic games, Athens, 1896
Olympic games, Los Angeles, 1932
Olympic games 1964*   ʟtitleʟ
OLYMPIC GAMES—REVIVAL, 1896–
Olympic games, Rome, 1960–
Olympic games (Winter) Innsbruck, 1964
Olympic games (Winter) Lake Placid, 1932

* In this title the date is filed as if it were spelled out ʟnineteen sixty-fourʟ because it is not part of a sequence.

D. Same heading with and without distinguishing numerals or dates. When the same name is used for more than one different thing (as a ship, balloon, etc.) or organization (as Ku Klux Klan) and one of them has no distinguishing numerals in its heading, arrange them in groups in the following order:

1) The heading with no numerals, without subheadings
2) The heading with no numerals, with all its corporate and subject subdivisions and longer entries beginning with the same name, interfiled

3) The heading with numerals, without subheadings
4) The heading with numerals, with all its corporate and subject subdivisions

Examples:

Explorer   ₁title₁
EXPLORER (ARTIFICIAL SATELLITE)
EXPLORER (BALLOON)
EXPLORER II (BALLOON)
An explorer comes home

KU KLUX KLAN
Ku Klux Klan in American politics
KU KLUX KLAN (1915–   )
KU KLUX KLAN (1915–   )—BIBLIOGRAPHY

United Nations
United Nations agreements
UNITED NATIONS—BUILDINGS
United Nations Conference on Trade and Employment . . .
United Nations.   Economic Affairs Dept.
UNITED NATIONS—YEARBOOKS
United Nations (1942–1945)
UNITED NATIONS (1942–1945)—SONGS AND MUSIC
United Nations (1942–1945)   Treaties, etc.

E. Numerals or dates designating parts of a whole or inclusive heading. When a series of numerals or dates designates parts of a whole and there are also alphabetical extensions of the inclusive heading, arrange the alphabetical group before the numerical group.

The following are typical examples of headings with entries for the whole and also for numbered or dated parts.

1. Chiefs of state. Disregard the name in parentheses that follows the dates.

Example:

U. S.   President
U. S.   President, Executive Office of the, *see* . . .
U. S.   President, 1789–1797 (Washington)

U. S.   President, 1801–1809 (Jefferson)
U. S.   President, 1953–1961 (Eisenhower)

2. Constitutions, charters, etc.

Example:

U. S.   Constitution
U. S.   CONSTITUTION—AMENDMENTS
U. S.   Constitution.   1st–10th amendments
U. S.   Constitution.   1st amendment
U. S.   Constitution.   4th amendment
U. S.   CONSTITUTION—SIGNERS

3. Legislatures

Example:

U. S.   Congress   ₁main and/or added entries₁
U. S.   CONGRESS
U. S.   Congress.   Aviation Policy Board
U. S.   CONGRESS—BIOGRAPHY
U. S.   Congress.   Committee on . . .
U. S.   Congress.   House   ₁main and/or added entries₁
U. S.   CONGRESS.   HOUSE
U. S.   Congress.   House.   Committee on . . .
U. S.   CONGRESS.   HOUSE—HISTORY
U. S.   Congress.   House.   Special Committee to . . .
U. S.   Congress.   Joint Committee on the Library
U. S.   CONGRESS—RULES AND PRACTICE
U. S.   Congress.   Senate   ₁main and/or added entries₁
U. S.   CONGRESS.   SENATE—ELECTIONS
U. S.   Congress.   Special Committee on . . .
U. S.   1st Congress, 1789–1791
U. S.   1ST CONGRESS, 1789–1791
U. S.   63d Congress, 1913–1915
U. S.   63d Congress, 1913–1915.   House
U. S.   63d Congress, 1913–1915.   Senate
U. S.   63d Congress, 1st session, 1913
U. S.   63d Congress, 1st session, 1913.   House
U. S.   63d Congress, 1st session, 1913.   Senate
U. S.   63d Congress, 2d session, 1913–1914
U. S.   63d Congress, 2d session, 1913–1914.   House

U. S.   63d Congress, 2d session, 1913–1914.   Senate
U. S.   63d Congress, 3d session, 1914–1915
U. S.   86th Congress, 1st session, 1959

4. Military units. Military units with distinctive names are arranged alphabetically by their names. Units beginning with a number (whether an Arabic or Roman numeral or spelled out) are arranged alphabetically by the word following the number, then numerically by the number. Regard the full name of the unit but disregard subdivisions or modifications of a unit except in relation to other headings under the unit with the same number.

Examples:

Connecticut Infantry.   Lyman's Regiment, 1757
Connecticut Infantry.   Putnam Phalanx
Connecticut Infantry.   1st Regt., 1762–1763
Connecticut Infantry.   1st Regt. (Militia)
Connecticut Infantry.   2d Regt., 1861
Connecticut Infantry.   Ward's Regiment, 1776–1777

U. S.   Army
U. S.   Army.   A. E. F., 1917–1920
U. S.   Army Air Forces
U. S.   Army Air Forces.   7th Air Force
U. S.   Army Air Forces.   8th Air Force
U. S.   Army Air Forces.   Air Service Command
U. S.   Army Air Forces.   303d Bombardment Group
U. S.   Army Air Forces.   305th Bombardment Group
    (Heavy)
U. S.   Army Air Forces.   386th Bombardment Group
U. S.   Army Air Forces.   11th Bombardment Squadron
U. S.   ARMY AIR FORCES—DRAMA
U. S.   Army Air Forces.   Flying Training Command
U. S.   Army and Navy Munitions Board
U. S.   Army.   First Army
U. S.   Army.   Third Army
U. S.   Army.   Fourth Army
U. S.   ARMY—BIOGRAPHY
U. S.   Army.   1st Cavalry
U. S.   Army.   1st Cavalry (Colored)
U. S.   Army.   3d Cavalry

U. S.	Army.	Continental Army
U. S.	Army.	II Corps
U. S.	Army.	IV Corps
U. S.	Army.	Corps of Engineers
U. S.	Army.	Engineer Amphibian Command
U. S.	Army.	148th Field Artillery
U. S.	Army.	148th Field Artillery. Battery C
U. S.	Army.	305th Field Artillery

37. Non-book material arrangement

Preliminary note. This rule provides for the arrangement of entries for non-book materials and for their integration with entries for books and book-like materials.

Many libraries maintain separate catalogs for non-book materials such as music, phonorecords, motion pictures, etc. Filing is easier if each category is kept separate. However, the cataloging rules for such materials are so designed that the resulting entries may be integrated with those for books.

A. General rule. Interfile entries for non-book materials in their alphabetical places with other entries. If the same heading occurs for both book and non-book materials, arrange entries for the non-book materials after those for the books. In relation to longer entries beginning with the same words consider only the part preceding the designation of physical medium in the non-book entry; do not alphabet by the designation. When there is more than one special category with the same heading, arrange the categories alphabetically by the designation of physical medium.

B. Music

Examples for rules without specific illustrations will be found in the Comprehensive examples, p. 79.

Note. Uniform titles[9] are frequently used in the cataloging of music. Like other uniform titles, they serve as a means of organizing the entries in a systematic manner. The special arrangement, however, can be achieved only with the application of the filing rules which are given below.

---

9. For definition of uniform title see footnote 5, p. 42.

1. **Basic rule.** Arrange all titles under a composer entry alphabetically (with minor exceptions for certain uniform titles as specified below), interfiling uniform titles with other titles and composer-title cross references.

2. **Singular and plural forms.** Interfile singular and plural forms of the names of musical forms, regardless of language (e. g., Sonata, Sonatas; Concerti, Concerto, Concertos), in the filing position of the singular.

3. **Numerals.** File numerals that designate sequences of compositions numerically.

4. **Punctuation.** Regard marks of punctuation in uniform titles that are identical up to the different punctuation mark. The filing sequence of these marks of punctuation is as follows:

1) Closing bracket

2) Semicolon

3) Period

4) Parentheses

5) Comma

6) No punctuation (longer titles)

Example:

[Concertos, organ, op. 7]
[Concertos, organ, op. 7; arr.]
[Concertos, organ, op. 7.   Selections]
[Concerto, organ, op. 7, no. 1, B♭ major]
[Concerti grossi, op. 6]   [longer title]
[Concerto grosso, op. 6, no. 1, G major]

5. **Elements following a period.** Interfile in one alphabetical file all elements that follow a period in a uniform title.

6. **Arrangement of entries under the same uniform title.** Arrange entries that are identical up to the end of the uniform title alphabetically by title page titles. When there are two or more editions with the same title, subarrange them by imprint dates, according to Rule 26B8.

7. **Different kinds of entries for the same title.** Regard the title portion of composer-title added entries, analytical entries made in the form of composer-title added entries, and composer-title

subject entries as a uniform title (except that the brackets are omitted). For the order of different kinds of entries under the same uniform title follow Rule 26B12.

8. Phonorecords—Music with uniform titles

a. General rule. When uniform titles are otherwise identical, arrange an entry for a phonorecord after the corresponding entry without a statement of physical medium. Do not alphabet by the word "Phonodisc," etc. in relation to words within the brackets of uniform titles.

Example:

    [La traviata]
    [La traviata] Phonodisc
    [La traviata. Libretto. English and Italian]
    [La traviata. Selections]
    [La traviata. Selections] Phonodisc

b. Arrangement of entries under the same uniform title. Arrange entries that are identical up to the end of the uniform title and term following the closing bracket alphabetically by transcribed titles. When there are two or more entries with the same title, subarrange alphabetically by the name of the record publisher, then alphabetically by the letter prefix and numerically by the record number.

Example:

Verdi, Giuseppe
    [Operas. Selections] Phonodisc.
    Arias. Columbia ML 5654. [1961]

    [Operas. Selections] Phonodisc.
    Arias. Columbia MS 6254. [1961]

    [Operas. Selections] Phonodisc.
    Baritone arias. RCA Victor LM 1932. [1955]

    [Operas. Selections] Phonodisc.
    Overtures. Angel Records ANG. 35676. [1960]

    [Operas. Selections] Phonodisc.
    Overtures. Mercury MG 50156. [1958]

c. **Different kinds of entries for the same title.** Arrange composer-title added entries for phonorecords and analytical entries made in the form of composer-title added entries in the group of phonorecords following the same title as a score. For the order of different kinds of entries under the same uniform title follow Rule 26B12.

Comprehensive examples for music, 37B:

Strauss, Johann
    ₜDie Fledermausₗ
    ₜDie Fledermaus. Englishₗ Phonodisc.
    ₜDie Fledermaus. Libretto. English & Germanₗ
    ₜDie Fledermaus. Overtureₗ
    ₜDie Fledermaus. Overtureₗ Phonodisc.
    ₜDie Fledermaus. Piano-vocal score. Englishₗ
    ₜDie Fledermaus. Waltzes; arr.ₗ Phonodisc.
    ₜDie Fledermaus (The bat: Park) Piano-vocal score. Englishₗ
    ₜDie Fledermaus (Golden Butterfly) Piano-vocal score. Englishₗ

Beethoven, Ludwig van, 1770–1827
    Letters.
    Rondo, for violin and piano, *see his* . . .
    ₜRondo, piano, op. 51, no. 1, C majorₗ
    ₜSonatas, pianoₗ

BEETHOVEN, LUDWIG VAN, 1770–1827
SONATAS, PIANO.
Fischer, Edwin
Ludwig van Beethovens Klaviersonaten.

Beethoven, Ludwig van, 1770–1827
    ₜSonatas, piano. Selectionsₗ

    ₜSonata, piano, no. 23, op. 57, F minorₗ
    Sonata. F moll. Op. 57. (Appassionata) Leipzig, Forberg ₜc1902ₗ

    ₜSonata, piano, no. 23, op. 57, F minorₗ Phonodisc.
    Sonata in F minor, op. 57 (Appassionata) Sonata in C major, op. 2, no. 3. RCA Victor LSC 2812. ₜ1965ₗ

[Sonata, piano, no. 23, op. 57, F minor] Phonodisc.
Sonata, no. 23, in F minor, op. 57 (Appassionata)
Sonata, no. 8, in C minor, op. 13 (Pathétique) RCA Victor
LM 1908. [1955]
    Beethoven, Ludwig van, 1770–1827
    Sonata, piano, no. 23, op. 57, F minor. Phonodisc.
Beethoven, Ludwig van, 1770–1827
[Sonata, piano, no. 17, op. 31, no. 2, D minor]
Phonodisc.
    Sonata no. 17, in D minor, op. 31, no. 2 ("Tempest")
    Sonata no. 23, in F minor, op. 57 ("Appassionata") RCA
    Victor LM 1964. [1956]
Beethoven, Ludwig van, 1770–1827
[Sonatas, violin & piano. Selections] Phonodisc.
Beethoven, Ludwig van, 1770–1827
Sonata pastorale, *see his* . . .
Beethoven, Ludwig van, 1770–1827
[Symphony, no. 6, op. 68, F major]
BEETHOVEN, LUDWIG VAN, 1770–1827
SYMPHONY, NO. 6, OP. 68, F MAJOR.
Beethoven, Ludwig van, 1770–1827
Ein Skizzenbuch zur Pastoralsymphonie, op. 68, und zu
den Trios, op. 70, 1 und 2.
Beethoven, Ludwig van, 1770–1827
[Symphony, no. 6, op. 68, F major] Phonodisc.

The symphony of life, letters by Ludwig van Beethoven.
[Works]
[Works. Selections; arr.]
[Works, chamber music. Selections]
[Works, piano. Selections]
BEETHOVEN, LUDWIG VAN, 1770–1827—
    BIBLIOGRAPHY
BEETHOVEN, LUDWIG VAN, 1770–1827—THEMATIC
    CATALOGS

C. Motion pictures and filmstrips
    1. General rule. Interfile entries for motion pictures and film-
strips in their alphabetical places with other entries. If there is an

identical entry for a book, arrange the entry for a motion picture or filmstrip after it. When there are entries with different designations arrange alphabetically by the designations.

Examples:

> Toward spiritual security
> Fallow, Wesner

> Toward statehood (Filmstrip)

> Toward the automatic factory
> Walker, Charles Rumford

> The emperor's new clothes
> Andersen, Hans Christian

> The emperor's new clothes (Filmstrip)   Society for
>   Visual Education, 1960.

> The emperor's new clothes (Motion picture)   Progress
>   Film, Munich. 1959.

2. Position in relation to longer entries. When there are longer entries beginning with the same word, arrange the entries for the non-book material before the longer entries, disregarding the parenthetical designation of physical medium in relation to the other entries.

Example:

> Hamlet, John

> Hamlet
> Shakespeare, William, 1564–1616
> > Editions of this work will be found under the author's
> name.

> Hamlet (Motion picture)
> Baylor Theater's Hamlet (Motion picture)

> Hamlet and Brownswiggle
> Reynolds, Barbara Leonard

3. Subarrangement under same title. Subarrange entries that are identical through the designation first alphabetically by name of producer, then chronologically by imprint date, then by any other distinguishing feature.

Example:

The challenge (Motion picture)   Audio production, 1959.

Challenge (Motion picture)   Florida State Alcoholic
    Rehabilitation Program . . .   1958

D. Phonorecords—Music without uniform titles and non-musical works. When there is no other entry for the same title, file the entry for the phonorecord in its alphabetical place. If there is another entry, file the entry for the phonorecord after the entry for the book, disregarding subtitles on both. When there are two or more phonorecord entries with the same title, subarrange alphabetically by the name of the record publisher, then numerically by the record number.

Examples:

Great operatic scenes.   ₍Phonodisc₎

    The great organizers
Dale, Ernest

Great poems of the English language.   ₍Phonodisc₎

Whitman, Walt
    Leaves of grass   ₍all editions of the book₎
    Leaves of grass.   ₍Phonodisc₎
    Memories of Lincoln.
    The song of myself (abridged)   ₍Phonodisc₎
    Songs of democracy.

E. Radio and television programs. Entries for the names of radio and television programs are filed according to the same rules as motion pictures and filmstrips (see 37C above).

Example:

    Americans at work
Paradis, Adrian A

Americans at work (Radio program)

APPENDIX

Initial articles
to be disregarded in filing

The following table lists definite and indefinite articles in various languages *in the nominative case only* (all genders and both numbers) which should be disregarded according to the rule for Articles (Rule 4). Under each language they are listed in the following order: Singular—masculine, feminine, neuter; Plural—same; an elided form follows its corresponding word or group of words; each article is listed only once under each language.

* before an indefinite article indicates that the same form is also used for the cardinal numeral "one," therefore care must be taken to distinguish the meaning.

Language	Definite article	Indefinite article
Dutch	De, Het, 't, 's[1]	*Een, Eene, 'n
English	The	A, An
French	Le, La, L', Les	*Un, *Une
German	Der,[2] Die, Das	*Ein, *Eine
Italian	Il, La, Lo, I, Gli, Gl', Le, L'	*Un, *Uno, *Una, *Un'
Norwegian (Riksmål)	Den, Det, De	*En, *Et
Norwegian (Nynorsk) (formerly called Landsmål)	Den, Det, Dei	*Ein, *Ei, *Eit
Spanish	El, La, Lo, Los, Las	*Un, *Una
Swedish	Den, Det, De	*En, *Ett

1. Disregard the Dutch " 's" when initial letter.
2. Disregard only when in the nominative case.

Index

References without designations are to rule numbers; those preceded by p. indicate pages; Ex. denotes reference to an example; references to notes, footnotes, etc. are so designated.

"A," as initial article, 4A
Abbreviations, 6
    "N. T." and "O. T." (Bible), 29G
    of geographical names, 6B
    of subject subdivisions, 6C
    see also Acronyms; Initials
"Abd" (in Oriental names), 15A3
Abridged editions, 26B8c
"Abu" (in Oriental names), 15A3
Accent marks, 2
Acronyms, 5E
Added entries
    interfiled with main entries,
      26B2
    see also Author-title added
      entries; Composer-title
      added entries
Additions to personal names, *see*
    Designations (additions
    to personal names)
"Al," "Āl" (at beginning of Arabic
    names), 15A2
"al-" (article in Oriental names)
    as initial article, 15A1
    within a name, 15A3
Alphabeting rule, basic, 1
Alternative titles, *see* Subtitles
American Indian names, 16

Ampersand (&), 8B
"An," as initial article, 4A
Analytical entries
    author, 26B10
    composer-title, 37B7
      phonorecords, 37B8c
    subject, 32B
    works about an author, 26C
    title, 33B1
"Ancient" (as subject subdivision),
    32E4
"And"
    in numerals, 9A
    supplied for "&," 8B
"and Company" (in corporate
    names), 23
Anglo-American Cataloging Rules,
    27, prelim. note; 29,
    note
Anonymous classics, 30
    see also Bible
Anonymous title entries, *see* Title
    main entries
Apostrophes
    in elisions, contractions, and
      possessives, 7
    in names with a prefix, 14

"Appellant," 26B3
   after geographical names, 31C
Appellatives,   *see*   Designations
      (additions   to   personal
      names)
Arabic names, 15A
Army units, 36E4
Articles, 4
   foreign elided, 7 .
   initial, 4A
      at beginning of a nickname
         or sobriquet, 17
      foreign   same   as   numeral
         "one," p. 83
      list of, p. 83
      prefixed   to   personal   and
         place names, 14
      Oriental names, 15A
      uncapitalized,   prefixed   to
         Islamic   and   Hebrew
         names, 15A1
   within a compound name, 13
   within   a   given   name   entry,
      25B1
   within an entry, 1B, 4B
   within an Oriental name, 15A3
Associations, *see* Societies, organ-
      izations, etc.
Author entries
   arrangement
      general rules, 26
      uniform title system, 27
   classic and voluminous authors,
      introd. notes to 26–27,
      p. 33; 27
   joint author [editor, etc.], 26B3
   order   of   different   kinds   of
      entries for the same title,
      26B12
   works about the author, 26A,
      26C
   works by the author, 26A–B
   see also Corporate entries
Author statement
   at beginning of title, 26B5
   "by" phrase, 26B4

Author-title . . . *see also* Composer-
      title . . .
Author-title added entries, 26B9,
      26B12
Author-title references, 35D
Author-title series entries, 34B
Author-title subject entries,
      26B11–12
Author's   name at beginning of
      title, 26B5

"B–17 Bomber," Ex., p. 13
"Bar" (in Oriental names), 15A3
Basic alphabeting rule, 1
Basic order, p. 1
Basic principle, p. 1
"Beethoven" (music title arrange-
      ment), Ex., p. 79
Belles-lettres, introd. notes to 26–
      27, p. 33
"Ben" (in Oriental names), 15A3
Bible, 29
   dates in headings, 29C
   headings changed in new cata-
      loging rules, 29, note
   numbered books, 29F
   parts of books, 29E
Bishop's see, 24
Brackets, uniform title enclosed in,
      27, prelim. note
Bureaus
   subheading   under   corporate
      names, 28B
   subheading under geographical
      names, 31D
Business firms, name entries be-
      ginning with a surname,
      23
Bynames, *see* Designations (addi-
      tions to personal names);
      Nicknames

"California" (place name), Ex.,
      p. 56
"Charles," Ex., p. 32

Date of publication—*continued*
editions arranged by, introd.
notes to 26–27, p. 33;
26B8
Dates
after personal names, 20D
alphabeted as spoken, 9
see also Chronological arrangement
"De"
dialect article, 12
prefix in proper names, 14
"Defendant," 26B3
after geographical names, 31C
Departments
subheading under corporate
names, 28B
subheading under geographical
names, 31D
Designations (additions to personal names)
in given name entries, 25
in surname entries, 20B, 20C1,
20D
Designations (showing relationship of heading to one
work), 26B3
Diacritical marks, 2
Dialect forms, 12
Dictionary catalog, 1C
Different kinds of entry under
same word, order of, 19
"Dr." (abbreviation), Ex., p. 7
Dynasty, name of, 22

"ed." (designation following heading), 26B3
Editions, 26B8
abridged, 26B8c
reprint, introd. notes to 26–27,
p. 34
title added entries—subarrangement, 33B2
various possible methods of

arrangement, introd.
notes to 26–27, p. 33
with different titles, 26B7,
26B8b
uniform title system, 27
"El" (Arabic), 15A2; Ex., p. 20
"El" (Spanish article prefixed to
names), Ex., p. 20
"el-" (article in Oriental names)
as initial article, 15A1
within a name, 15A3
Elided prefix, names with, 14
Elisions, 7
Entries under same word, order
of, 19
Entry, *see* Added entries; Analytical entries; Main entries; Series entries; etc.
Explanatory notes and references,
see References

Family names, 22
Figures, *see* Numerals
Filmstrips, 37C
"(Firm)," etc. (in corporate
names), 23
Firm names, beginning with a surname, 23
Foreign articles, *see* Articles
Foreign languages
entries in, 1A
modified letters, etc., 2
Foreign prepositions and pronouns, elided, 7
Forenames
in firm names, 23
surnames arranged by, 20B–C
see also Given name entries
"FORTRAN," Ex., p. 7

Geographical names
abbreviations, 6B
arrangement of, *see* Place arrangement
compound, 13

Geographical names—*continued*
  followed by a personal name or
    personal title, 24
  with prefix, 14A
  "Germany" (place name), Ex.,
    p. 57
Given name entries, 25
  filing position, 25B
  numerals in, 25A
Governmental divisions, official,
  31D
Governments with same name,
  31E
"El Greco," Ex., p. 23

"ha-," "he-" (article in Hebrew
    names)
  as initial article, 15A1
  within a name, 15A3
Hebrew names, 15A
"Henry VIII" (title), Ex., p. 13
"Homer"
  arrangement under author, Ex.,
    p. 40
  filing position, Ex., p. 32
"House of," 22
Humorous forms, 12
Hyphenated words, 11
Hyphens
  in American Indian names, 16
  in Chinese names, 15B2
  in compound names, 13, 21
  in names with a prefix, 14
  Oriental names, 15

"I," as an initial and as a Chinese
    surname, 15B3
"Ibn" (in Oriental names), 15A3
"illus." (designation following
    heading), 26B3
Imprint date, *see* Date of publi-
    cation
"inc." (in corporate names), 23
Indefinite article same as numeral
    "one," p. 83

Indian names, American, 16
Initial articles, *see* Articles—
    initial
Initialisms, 5
  forming a word, 5E
Initials, 5
  acronyms, 5E
  as abbreviations, 6A
    for geographical names, 6B
  forename, 20B–C
    in corporate name entries
      beginning with a sur-
      name, 23A
  inverted, 5C
  standing for names of organi-
    zations, 5B
  subarrangement of entries un-
    der same initials, 5D
Institutions, *see* Societies, organi-
    zations, etc.
Inverted headings
  place names, 31B
  subjects, 32C
Islamic names, 15A
Italics, p. x

Japanese names, 15B
"joint author [editor," etc.] (desig-
    nation following head-
    ing), 26B3
Jurisdictions with same name,
    31E

Kings, *see* Sovereigns

Legislatures, 36E3
"Life" (periodical title), Ex., p. 65
"Lincoln" (place name), Ex., p. 55
"London" (place name), Ex., p. 56
"ltd." (in corporate names), 23

"M."
  abbreviation, 6A
  initial, Ex., p. 6

"M' ", "Mac," "Mc" (prefixes in
    names), 14B
Magazine titles, *see* Periodical
    and newspaper titles
Main entries
    interfiled with added entries,
        26B2
    order of different kinds of en-
        tries for the same title,
        26B12
Marks, diacritical, 2
"Mc" (prefix in names), 14B
"Medieval" (as subject subdivi-
    sion), 32E4
Military units, 36E4
"Modern" (as subject subdivi-
    sion), 32E4
Modified letters, 2
Mohammedan . . . *see* Islamic . . .
Motion pictures, 37C
"Mr.," as abbreviation, 6A
"Mrs."
    as abbreviation, 6A
    in author headings, 20B–D
Music, 37B
    arrangement of entries under
        the same uniform title,
        37B6
    phonorecords, 37B8b
    phonorecords
        with uniform titles, 37B8
        without uniform titles, 37D
Musical forms, singular and plural
    interfiled, 37B2

"N. T." (abbreviation for New
    Testament), 29G
Names
    American Indian, 16
    Arabic, 15A
    Chinese, 15B
    compound, *see* Compound
        names
    corporate, *see* Corporate en-
        tries; Corporate names

firm, 23
    geographical, *see* Geographical
        names
    Hebrew, 15A
    Islamic, 15A
    Japanese, 15B
    Oriental, 15
    spelled differently, 18
    with prefix, 14
"New York" (place name), Ex.,
    p. 55
Newspaper titles, *see* Periodical
    and newspaper titles
Nicknames, 17
Noblemen
    given name entries, 25
    headings consisting of place
        name combined with
        personal names, 24
    surname entries, 20B–D
Non-book material, 37
Numerals, 9
    following given names in head-
        ings, 25A
    following given names in titles,
        9B, 25B2; footnote 6,
        p. 44
    in music titles, 37B3
    in names of military units, 36E4
    in names of things, 9C, 36D
    "one" same as indefinite arti-
        cle, p. 83
    table of, 9A1
Numerical arrangement, 36
    Bible—chapters and verses,
        29E
    Bible—numbered books, 29F
    see also Chronological arrange-
        ment

"O. T." (abbreviation for Old
    Testament), 29G
Offices
    subheading under corporate
        names, 28B

"Who's who" (serial title), Ex.,
    p. 66
Word by word arrangement, 1B
Words spelled in different ways,
    10
    see also Spelling, variations in
Words written in different ways,
    11

Works
    about an author, 26A, 26C
    by an author, 26A–B
        uniform title system, 27
        complete, *see* Complete works
        music, 37B1

"Ye," 12